Thirty years ago Bishop Jo[...] about the meaning of the creation stories in the first chapters of the Bible. It was a book which quickly became famous. Now, thirty years later he has written a whole new book on this same theme; and this is a book which will surely become even more renowned. It is a work full of the reflection and experience of a life-time, written with the clarity and power of a C. S. Lewis; a book to be pondered and pondered again.

Canon A. M. Allchin

This is another of John Davies' fine biblical expositions: in his hands the creation is presented in all its gospel significance. The reflections and questions for discussion make this a book which is accessible to us all as one of the most useful and usable study outlines available on the opening chapters of Genesis.

Peter Selby
Bishop of Worcester

Full of refreshing insights about the creation stories of Genesis, scientifically informed, and with practical suggestions for those who try to *do* theology.

Dr Jenifer M. Baker
F. I. Biol

John Davies was Bishop of Shrewsbury from 1987 to 1994. Previously, he spent many years in rural parish and city university ministry in South Africa, Wales and England. He is a former principal of the College of the Ascension in Birmingham and a Residentiary Canon of St Asaph Cathedral.

The author of numerous books and Bible study guides, he lives on the border between England and Wales, near Oswestry. For a number of years he served as a member of the local council, and with his wife Shirley is an Associate of the Iona Community.

Also by the same author:

Be Born in Us Today:
The meaning of the Incarnation for today

The Crisis of the Cross:
An exploration of the Easter story

God at Work

Creation then and now
– a practical exploration

John Davies

CANTERBURY
PRESS
Norwich

To Shirley, constantly creative
as woman, wife, mother, nain

© John Davies 2001

First published in 2001 by the Canterbury Press Norwich
(a publishing imprint of Hymns Ancient & Modern Limited
a registered charity)
St Mary's Works, St Mary's Plain
Norwich, Norfolk, NR3 3BH

British Library Cataloguing in Publication Data

A catalogue record of this book is available
from the British Library

ISBN 1–85311–402–2

Typeset by Regent Typesetting, London
Printed in Great Britain by
Bookmarque, Croydon, Surrey

Contents

The earth is the Lord's and all that is in it:
the world and its people belong to the Lord

Introduction

This is a book about everything. Everything includes you.

The theme throughout this book is the great statement at the beginning of Psalm 24: *The earth is the Lord's, and all that is in it: the world and its people belong to the Lord.* We are here because God is at work. God is our maker; all that we possess is on loan from our Creator.

This theme is developed in the first three chapters of Genesis, the first book of the Bible. These interpret to us the creation of the universe. The universe is immensely large, immensely complex and immensely old, so I am not going to be able to discuss it properly in a book of this size. There are many questions that I will just not be able to deal with at all.

All I can offer are the reflections of one man, now growing old. If you find something here which speaks to you, fine; if not, do look elsewhere. Genesis 1–3 are, I suppose, the most discussed parts of the Hebrew Scriptures (which Christians call the Old Testament), and I cannot possibly refer to all the wisdom which they have generated across the centuries. Instead I offer a few ways of making connections with our situation today. We read these stories of God at work in his world, in the hope that they will help us to recognize God at work in his world today.

Thirty years ago, I wrote a book about these chapters of Genesis.[1] This present book is almost entirely different. The text of Genesis remains the same; however, I have changed a lot. For example, 30 years ago, I was a South African exile, unexpectedly cast up on Britain's shores, homeless and jobless. It was the most miserable and insecure period of my life. Now I live, as I have lived for 20 years, on the border between Wales and England; I cross that border virtually every day. Thirty years ago, one of my intentions was to help people to see how important the Christian understanding of creation had been to us in the struggle against the ideology of apartheid. Apartheid, as a political programme, is now past history; but this text is, I believe, still very important to human beings as we struggle against slavery and racial injustice.

Thirty years ago, biology was bubbling over with excitement from the DNA discovery. Now, the results of that discovery are in routine use in forensic laboratories, and a vast range of new exploration has been taking place in the fields of astronomy and of fundamental physics – an ordinary reader like myself is left feeling somewhat disabled. Thirty years ago, people across the Western world were gripped by a fear of nuclear war between the great powers of East and West; now, people are still afraid: but the fear is of another disaster like that of Chernobyl, and of the cost of decommissioning of nuclear installations, which we are bequeathing to many generations of our descendants.

Thirty years ago, we could point to the irony that we could fly cargoes of wealthy people half-way across the planet at supersonic speeds, but were unable to provide housing for the poorest members of the community. The problems, we should note, were spiritual, not technical or economic; it was *motivation* which determined what we did and what we did not do, and motivation is a matter of the will, entirely a spiritual matter. Now the first part of that comparison looks sick; Concorde has been grounded, due to the tragic and fatal crash in 2000; but the second part of the comparison remains firmly in place.[2]

Thirty years ago, I was writing as a man in the middle of his working life, with three children at school. Now I am a pensioner, with five grandchildren; I have had 30 more years of living with a continually creative woman, and of realizing what it means to be male; and the next main appointment that I anticipate (although it is not written in my diary!) is death. All these points affect the way I approach a text such as the first three chapters of Genesis, and they all have echoes later in this book.

But first, I need to make two preliminary statements which have a bearing on the whole book. First, science is successful at analysing and creating categories. The opening chapter of Genesis appears to be working in a way similar to some departments of science, and so we may be tempted to expect to find scientific truth in it. I share the fascination of the intellectual quest of the scientific mind, but this is not theology. Theology, if it is to be true to its fundamental purpose, and to the purposes for which Genesis was written, is about discerning the mind, character and purpose of God. How is God at work among us? How do we share in his work? A theology that does not motivate us to get involved with the struggle for God's will and God's authority is a very deficient theology. A theology that does not inspire the imagination is as deficient as a theology that cuts corners in intellectual honesty. A theology that does not lead to worship of the Creator is failing in its task of re-ordering our values; true worship leads us to recognize God at work, as Lord over all the secondary authorities and deceptive power-systems which claim the allegiance of human hearts. A theology that does not stand alongside the poor and disadvantaged, the disabled and exiled, is a deficient theology; it misrepresents the God who, in the manger and cross of Christ, has shown us where he is to be sought and found on earth. Genesis is theology; and I hope that this book is theology too.

God at Work

Secondly, as I have already mentioned, this book is concerned with the first three chapters of Genesis. These represent two very distinct traditions of literature, but unfortunately our customary division into chapters obscures this. The first section or tradition runs from chapter 1 verse 1 to chapter 2 verse 4a. A quite different tradition then starts. For the sake of convenience, I refer to 'chapter 1' and 'chapter 2'; but please note that 'chapter 1' includes the first three verses of chapter 2. This is important, as will be clear when we come to the 'seventh day' in the chapter 1 scheme of things. Without the seventh day (in chapter 2, verses 1 to 4a) the first six days lose their basic aim and location. Both traditions derive from the Hebrew people's experience of suffering. Chapter 1, with its majestic picture of an increasingly complex universe, represents some of the most mature spirituality of the Hebrew people: it arises out of the dreadful experience of exile; it is a defiant statement of the eternal faithfulness of God, and a counterblast to the oppressive theologies of the nations at whose hands they had suffered so much. The second and third chapters come from a much earlier period of Israelite history and spirituality. They come from a community which had, not so long ago, known the cruelty of slavery. They knew what it meant to be a community created by God. The position of the book of Genesis – first in the Bible – is its logical place, because it is about the beginning, and 'Genesis' simply means 'beginning'. However, the experience of Exodus came first. It was a community which knew and remembered Exodus that created Genesis. Because they were themselves a nation created by God out of slavery, they could see that the same God was the creator of all things. I shall return to this process in more detail at the appropriate places in the text.

Theologians speak of the inspiration of scripture; they usually assume that this inspiration comes to an individual person writing alone. Scholars think this way, because in most cases they are themselves individuals writing alone. But much of scripture comes from communities, and the community is where inspiration happens. Its insights are transmitted by the scribe, writing on behalf of the community. So in this book I refer to 'the authors' of chapter 1 and to 'the authors' of chapters 2 and 3. (Probably more than one tradition and community is in fact represented in chapters 2 and 3, anyway.) I also am a scribe, transmitting some of the insights of many people with whom I have worked in study-groups on these texts, both in this country and in South Africa. They have been both inspired and inspiring; they are the real authors of this book.

So I invite you to study Genesis to try to work with its primary message. In making a scientific study of, for example, a tennis racket, it would be necessary to analyse the materials, to calculate the weights and tensions of the structure and to work out the economics of production. However, you will not find out what the tennis racket really *is* unless you get involved in the game. The 'game' of Genesis is, as it ever was, the call to work with God in his work of creating and re-creating his world. This means not only trying to understand more about *how* the universe works – which is a proper concern of science – but also asking *why* there should be a universe at all. Some would say that this is a meaningless question, to which no answer is possible; and there is no way of proving that they are wrong. But biblical faith does lead to an answer, an answer which is not just an intellectual statement but a call to put our energies into working with the purposes of the Creator: for Christians, this means following Jesus, Son of God, through whom all things were made.

The purpose of this sort of study is not to tell you things that you do not know, but to encourage you to look in a new way at things that you already know. The important thing is to let the story make connections with your own experience and your own situation. No one else can do this for you. You are the expert on your own experience. All that a book like this can do is to offer a few hints.

I have ended each chapter not with a prayer but with a place to visit, where some of the ideas of the chapter could be used in your own reflection on the creation. Most of the places I am suggesting are in or around North Wales, as that is the part of the world that I happen to know best. What matters, however, is not the specific place, but the type of place, and the type of reflection that you might discover there.

I hope that this book will be of interest not only to people reading it alone, but also to groups of Christian disciples who are seeking to work out their obedience to God in the life of their local church and community. The text of the New Revised Standard Version is provided, but members of study-groups would do well to bring their own versions with them to their meeting: at several points, there are valuable alternative translations available, and no single version has a monopoly of wisdom in the interpretation. The speeches are clearly identified in the printed text, so that, when the text is read aloud in the group, the speaking parts can be shared out among different readers. This is especially appropriate in Genesis 3 (see chapters 7 and 8 below).

I have attached a few questions to each of the chapters to suggest lines of exploration, but the primary questions, before dealing with these detailed questions, should be: *What connections do we see between this text and our own experience? How are we seeing the Creator God at work in his world?* When you reach the specific questions at the end of each chapter, if the group is large, split up into small teams and tackle one question each. Then, at the end, come together and share your ideas and conclusions.

This book is intended mainly to be about practical discipleship and obedience to God. That is what the original text is designed and valued for. It shows us God at work. But it is very easy with this subject to get diverted into all sorts of issues about what did and what didn't happen 4000 or 15 billion years ago. So it would be a good idea to aim at making specific practical decisions as a result of each phase of study, and to record these, so that, where appropriate, they can be passed on as recommendations or questions to other church groups, or other authorities.

Finally, there are two poets who have been valuable companions to me in the pilgrimage of working with the struggles and the connectednesses of creation. They are, in my view, the two most deeply searching Welsh poets, writing in English, of the twentieth century. David Jones was formed by his Flintshire background and by his experience of the trenches in the Great War; his long poem, *The Anathemata,* marvellously draws together primeval inorganic matter and the universal significance of the Christian mysteries. And no one has wrestled with prayer amid the coldness and randomness of things studied by science with such authority as R. S. Thomas. In a small way, this book could be a pointer to the far greater wisdom that you could gain from these two minds.[3]

John Davies
Gobowen
All Saints' Day 2000

1

Creating a Universe

*In the beginning when God created the heavens and the
earth, the earth was a formless void and darkness
covered the face of the deep, while a wind from God**
swept over the face of the waters. Then God said,*
   'Let there be light';
*and there was light. And God saw that the light was
good; and God separated the light from the darkness.
God called the light Day, and the darkness he called
Night. And there was evening and there was morning,
the first day.*

Genesis 1:1–5

Genesis states that God was in the beginning. God's activity
is the beginning.

God has no beginning. God is in the beginning. If we
could know exactly what the beginning was, that knowledge would simply push the frontier one stage further
back. To ask what was the beginning is like asking what is
beyond space: if we had access to it, it would cease to be
'beyond'.

So what was God doing before he made heaven and
earth? St Augustine's answer was that there could be no
'before', because 'before' means that there must be some

---

* Or *while the Spirit of God* or *while a mighty wind.*

way of reckoning time, and time itself is part of the created order.[1]

According to most modern students of physics, in the beginning was the Big Bang, in which the basic constituents of the universe were formed. Here we meet the implications of time in a dramatic and unimaginable way. It was an event occupying zero space and a tiny fraction of a second, 15 or so billion years ago, at colossal temperature. The universe was simple, a rapidly expanding ball of energy. After three minutes, the universe had cooled down to a mere thousand million degrees, and there was sufficient stability for the proportions of hydrogen and helium to form which have remained in place ever since. What has happened since the Big Bang is, in principle, knowable. But before it? People who believe in God can say that before the creation of the universe, in whatever manner, God was. But this does not provide an answer to the questions of the physicist. To the questions, 'Who made potatoes?', 'Where do babies come from?' or 'From where do ducks get webbed feet?', and so on, it is easy to answer 'God'. But does this word help at all? Is it anything more than a noise to make when we have no more specific answer? Is there any way of checking whether such an answer is true or false, or indeed whether it has any real meaning? Does it supply any new knowledge?

For the people of the Hebrew Scriptures, 'God' was not a means of giving an answer to otherwise unanswerable questions. 'God' was not a distant unmoved mover, or an explanation for intellectual scientific puzzles. For the Hebrews, God was one who had met them and worked with them in their own immediate history. God had made them a nation; he had delivered them from Egypt; he had shown himself to be on the side of people who had been oppressed and enslaved by a powerful empire. He had met them in their experience of chaos and darkness, and had made them a new community. This was the God whom they believed in as they tried to make sense of their own experience. From this experience, they worked back to the belief that this same God had been at work in the formation of the whole human race, the whole planet, the whole universe. So, while we may find the researches of physicists and cosmologists immensely interesting, intellectually and emotionally inspiring, they will not necessarily tell us about the most important characteristics of God in the way that God is known in the traditions of Jewish and Christian communities. Some scientists find that their studies do illuminate their faith in God; others find that their studies strengthen their conviction that there is no God and that there cannot be. In both cases, we need to insist that the God who is being discussed is the God who delivers the slave, takes the side of the poor and gives voice to the refugee. If not, we are not talking about the God of the Scriptures, the God who raised the crucified victim Jesus from the dead. The poor, the slave and the refugee have the right to ask us, as we talk about God the Creator, 'Has your God anything to offer us?'

God is the subject of the first verb in this story, and of most of the verbs in the first chapter of Genesis. The Scripture speaks of the one God who is the origin and the destiny of the universe, the master and critic of everything that is. It speaks of his purpose in creating the universe and in bringing it into relationship with himself. It speaks of his power over the earth, and his authority over history. But the community that produced and treasured this first chapter of Genesis was not merely looking back on the past from a comfortable or successful present. This celebration of the orderly and secure purpose of God was generated during a further time of distress and disorder, in the experience of the exile of the people of Israel in Babylon, in the sixth century BC. Once again, they were rootless and homeless, alienated from the land and from the work by which wealth could be created from the land. In Babylon, they heard an epic story of the creation of the world which was in common currency at the time. They took from this story many of the cosmological details which we find in Genesis chapter 1: for example, the chaos of darkness and water; the first creation of light, the division of the waters by a kind of dome. But in the Babylonian original, heaven and earth, the abyss and chaos, exist from the first. Then gods come into being; one of these gods, Marduk, arises as a champion, defeats Chaos and divides her into pieces. The Hebrews, exiles under a cruel regime, took over many of the ideas and words from the culture of their oppressors, and made from them the framework of their new statement of creation. Into the centre of the pagan framework, the Hebrews put a totally different picture of God: a God who not only made things but declared them to be good, a God who not only exerted power over creation but loved it. They 'baptized' pagan things. Later, Christians did the same sort of thing, when they took over and blessed old wells such as Holywell, and when they modified stories about old deities, weaving them into their honouring of Christian saints such as Brigit and Beuno, claiming them into their central obedience to Christ.[2] In our own day, we hear new stories of creation, from the culture of scientific investigation. In faith, we receive these as providing new language for expressing the central commitment of our belief, in God as Creator, Redeemer and Sanctifier. In a new way, we are seeing God at work.

The Hebrews, at this stage of their history, had good reason to disbelieve in the love of God for them; indeed, they wrote many psalms of complaint and perplexity to express their sense that God had deserted them. However, they made this majestic statement of their fundamental commitment to the belief that they were both created and loved. They owed their existence to a deliberate act of will by a good Creator, who made a decision and announced it. We, and the whole of the rest of creation, are not merely an accidental product of a God who does not really care about us. This is a proclamation of defiance; it is a rejection of the cultural assumptions of the powerful and the overlord. Indeed, it flies in the face of immediate experience. Experience suggests that we are caught in a muddle of conflicting authorities, rivalling and falling over each other in their attempts to dominate us. Experience suggests that the stories of the disordered collections of gods in the Babylonian or Greek or Norse mythologies are true to reality. Experience suggests that each group has its own god and its own ideology, its own form of justice which fits the interests of the most powerful members. If we feel, deep down, that our own presence in this world, and the presence of the world around us, are essentially valueless, it will make good sense to believe that the material universe has come into being through conflict and murder, fragmentation and curse. In that case, salvation will happen if we can escape from this material world. This is, I believe, the most widespread misunderstanding of Christian hope in these days. Many Christians expect that, if there is salvation at all, it will take us out of the present scene of material things, of politics and finance and sex, and take us into a totally different scene. This sort of attitude has crept into many faces of Christian spirituality. Indeed, the very word 'spirituality' means, for some people, a refuge from the things of this 'ordinary' world. This will give good religious sanction for my own self-rejection, for my own refusal of my created nature. I will be satisfied to feel that it is wicked of me to be me. Because the basic stuff of me is founded in conflict and curse, I need not grow into maturity. I can rest in my sense that what I am is my fate. I can rest in the assumption that the same is true of my fellow human beings. I can reject them because of their obvious faults. I need not do anything to improve their conditions or to make reconciliation. I can be a passive victim. I can let myself, and other people, be pushed around by the more powerful; I can let them tell me what is good for me and what I can and cannot do. In short, this sort of mythology is very attractive to those who want to control other people and keep them in their place. The majestic figure of the one God of creation, who forms the world in love and justice and creates human beings in his image – such a God is the one whom Jews and Christians worship. Such a God inspires us to identify the powers of chaos and darkness and to believe that they have met their master. Here, in the opening words of the Bible, is the uncompromising statement that there is one God, one justice, one purpose. We celebrate this God in our worship. We recognize that this God has authority over us and claims our commitment. Our worship defines our value-system. You are God, we praise you: you are the Lord, and we acclaim you. And all the other authorities which seek to claim our obedience, and scare us into submission by coercion or bribery, they all have to recognize and yield to the one God who is the God of the powerful and the powerless alike.

The first chapter of Genesis is not just a theological statement. It is a hymn of praise. There have been many commentaries on it, by many distinguished theologians all down the centuries, all writing in serious prose. But, to my mind, the best of all commentaries was written not by a recognized theologian but by Josef Haydn; his oratorio, *The Creation*, demonstrates that this sort of truth needs not only to be argued but to be sung.

The Bible's statements are not offered as contributions to scientific research. Historical or cosmological theories or discoveries cannot prove or disprove them. Equally, the Bible's statements are not supposed to tell the scientists what they ought to be finding. Intellectual study has its own rights. Scientists have the duty to make experiments and judgements which are in accordance with their particular disciplines; they are not called to assent to ready-made answers supplied by theologians or anyone else. If they find a point where something happens which they cannot explain in their own terms, they are not called to slide in the word 'God' to provide the answer. This especially applies in the questions about the beginning of things. Indeed, as Christian believers, we have to insist that if 'God' is not necessary to account for the maintenance of the cosmic structure, 'God' should not be brought in to account for its origin. Our belief in God as Creator means not only that God made all things but that he makes all things – including ourselves. God is not known, primarily, in terms of those matters which we cannot explain; what was inexplicable for the last generation has a way of being explained in the next. 'God' is a new way of comprehending things which are, already, to some extent explicable. God is not a device to compensate us for what we do not know; God is a new way of knowing what we already do know. If this were not so, every new thing that we know would be one less thing to know about God: but the more we are aware of our own experience, the more sensitive we are to our environment, and the more there is to say about God.

The earth was a formless void. Can you visualize formlessness? Whatever picture you try to make, it will involve some sort of shape or substance. Haydn made a remarkable attempt in the 'Representation of Chaos' in *The Creation*. 'Chaos', for Haydn, is not a condition where everything is rushing around in mad disorder; it is simply a condition where nothing really *is*. The music is full of shifts and vagueness: a cadence seems to approach but never arrives, because the music goes wandering off in another direction, which itself turns out to be illusory. The scene is not 'chaotic' in the usual sense of the word; it is a profound study of the instability which, according to Genesis, is the primal condition into which creation can break. I find that this makes a lot of sense. But it perhaps does not do justice to the violence which is also suggested in the text, a violence mirrored in the story of the massive cosmic explosion of the Big Bang. For a musical interpretation of this, listen to the much more catastrophic account of 'Chaos' which John Tavener makes in his *Fall and Resurrection*.

Christian teachers have often stressed the doctrine that God created the universe out of nothing. One reason for this tradition was to oppose the heretical idea, which was widely canvassed in the early centuries of the Christian movement, that the material world was created by a bad god and that salvation was to be found by getting away from it all. This stress on creation out of nothing also tells us that God's work is not simply a matter of reshaping basic material supplied to him from some other source; God is truly unconditioned, he supplies his own materials. But it should not lead us into thinking that God's creative work could happen only at the first beginning, when there was plenty of nothing to work on. The Bible does not speak much of a creation out of nothing (the nearest that we get to this idea in Scripture is in 2 Maccabees 7:28). What the Bible does tell us is that creation is the task of bringing order out of chaos. God sorts out the various components of chaos; he names them and distinguishes them, and, later, he calls his human creatures to share in the task. The final goal of all this is not a universe made up from lots of things made out of nothing but a complex harmony of beings brought into reconciliation with each other. This is the image of the Body in St Paul's teaching, and the image of the City in the book of Revelation.

Creation means getting involved with this chaos. Jesus, for instance, lived his first 30 years within the chaos, the social and political disorder and the religious mess of the Palestine of his upbringing. When he started to make a creative move, it was not out of this confusion but deeper into it. He joined the traditional figure of John the Baptist; he was taken down deeper into his community, down into the muddy waters of Jordan, at the lowest point on his nation's territory. Only after this immersion into the disorder of his contemporary circumstance did he take up a creative ministry of his own. He spent most of the years of his ministry in the religious and political confusion of Galilee, and the last hours of his incarnate life were in the even greater chaos of the Jerusalem of Pilate and Caiaphas. It was dark over the whole land on a certain Friday afternoon. Christ is crucified at the storm-centre of history; in his victory he overcomes darkness and all its powers. It is from this encounter with chaos at its most concentrated that we claim our salvation, a salvation which is not just for those who hear the story at a comfortable distance but also for those who themselves live within the chaos. Chaos and darkness remain; but their terror is overcome when we enter them in the company of one who is alongside us and has been there before us. He conquers hell by descending into it. If you want to find creation happening, look among the places of chaos and crucifixion. For some of Christ's followers, those who are set where they meet most potently the spiritual and social agonies of the world, the most appropriate blessing may be: 'Go forth into hell in peace, for your Master has mastered even it.'

Chaos is there, but it does not do anything. There is no myth of chaos; it is not personified. The same is true of darkness. Nothing is said about where they come from. They are not positive things; they are absences. An absence does not have to be created; it is an area where creativity has not yet happened. But darkness and chaos are. They have names. God's word recognizes them. For the Hebrews, darkness and chaos took their meaning not from speculation but from historical social experience. Chaos was something that they had known as a slave-community in Egypt, where they had been forced to make bricks without straw.

They had been released from that oppression, and this was their creation.

The spirit of God swept over the face of waters. This is the traditional translation. (In Hebrew, as in Greek and many modern languages, there is one word which means 'breath' or 'wind' or 'spirit', and it is impossible to be sure which meaning is intended in this sentence.) The Spirit of God is the Holy Spirit, the Spirit who inspired the prophets, the Spirit who animated Jesus, the Spirit who came on the Apostles at Pentecost, the Spirit who comes on us in baptism. This Spirit, according to traditional understanding, is not limited to human life and interest. This same Spirit was present, waiting, brooding, at the very beginning of things. God's word came as a command, from outside the created thing; but God's Spirit was already inside, in the process itself. God's Spirit was at work in the very beginning of creation. The same Spirit is at work in each of us, linking us directly to that original creative moment. The 15 billion years are, after all, not such a long time. The purpose of the Spirit is not to give us good religious feelings, but to make us sharers in the work of creation, and of renewing the creation. Our baptism in the water of creation makes us members of the Spirit's enterprise of renewing the face of the earth.

It is God's nature to create. But creation is not some sort of automatic result of God's existence. Rather, there has to be a specific initiative from God. The creation is called into existence by God, as a deliberate act of will. God wants the universe to be. He wants us to be. He makes room for something other than himself. He limits himself; he makes space for the creation to be. The root meaning of the word which we usually translate as 'Saviour' is one who gives space to those who do not have space. Creator and Saviour are the same God.

God speaks; he calls us into life. 'God said'; this is the

first main verb in the original text of the Bible. God's word is the first event.

Let there be light. Light is not only a thing which is seen. It is the means by which all things, including itself, are seen. Here in Genesis, it appears as the first creation, before all other things, including the structures which convey light. Although this is not an attempt to provide what we would call a scientific account of the origins of the universe, we may reasonably detect ways in which it does echo the patterns discovered by scientists. For instance, they tell us that the universe was at first simple and uncomplicated. Then gradually it became more and more diversified. Genesis tells us of a process of increasing precision and definiteness. The boundaries of chaos are pushed back by the advance of order and pattern. Whatever you choose to call the most basic distinction of all, whether you call it the distinction between light and darkness, positive and negative, protons and electrons, knowledge and ignorance, here this basic distinction appears. It is called the first day of creation. It is good. It is a gracious miracle. The birth of light is a moment of quiet, but also a moment of splendour. There is no more dramatic moment in the whole of music than the unadorned breakthrough of Haydn's chorus of 'And there was ... Light', in *The Creation*.

Light is positive. Its appearance is the commencement of the first day, and its reappearance after a period of darkness is the completion of the first day. Genesis does not speak, as we do, of 'morning and evening'. This story refers all the time to 'evening and morning'. The day begins and ends in light. Night has its name, its permission to be. But darkness can only interrupt light; it cannot master it.

Order emerges from disorder. This is what can be seen and celebrated. But, according to the laws of physics, this can be only part of the story. The universe as a whole is moving from order to disorder. If order increases in one part, disorder will be increasing in another part. Or, in other language, darkness has its kingdom. Astronomers are suggesting that 90% or more of the universe may be made of non-luminous 'dark matter'; unless there is this enormous amount of matter that can be detected only by its gravitational effect, there is no way of accounting for the formation of galaxies within the universe's 15-billion-year timescale. Darkness is allowed to be. It may be much more extensive than we have realized. But light still remains the positive power. Light is the gift by which seeing and reckoning and travelling are possible. The creation of order and of light discloses the positive nature of God and of God's purpose for us.

At the same time, there is a place within the providence of God for the darkness, the night, the shadow. In our creed, we confess faith in God who is maker not only of the visible but also of the invisible. Our individual formation is in the dark, between conception and birth. The mysterious workings of our bodies are in the dark. The seed grows secretly in the dark. It was from the darkness that God spoke to Moses in giving the Ten Commandments.[3] We need to recognize and work with this darkness, even when we feel that it is opposing the light which is the primary gift of God. The darkness can give space. It can provide a relief from the relentless demand of the light, of the shadowless neon tube shining for 24 hours a day, of the intellectual tyranny which demands always to be correct and rational. One of the simplest forms of torture is for the prisoner to be kept in a room where the light is never switched off. David Jones, the twentieth-century Welsh poet who was so conscious of the claims of the hidden languages of the land, made the prayer to Our Lady, the 'queen of otherness':

> In the bland megalopolitan light,
>   where no shadow is by day or by night,
>   be our shadow.[4]

This was 'the first day'. When we think of time, and especially when we recall some special period or moment – such as a millennium year – even sophisticated people forget about clocks and watches and statistics; rather, we think of time in terms of what it contains. This was the Hebrew way: the 'day of the Lord' was not a 24-hour period on a calendar but the time of God's specific activity. The 'days' of creation are all 'days' like this, phases when God is seen as creator and judge. Each 'day' brings a new differentiation, a new category; it is a phase within which there is a distinct new beginning and a distinct sense of completeness, a time within which a job can be done and assessed. This sense that things proceed in phases is not, in principle, incompatible with what we learn from modern cosmology. After the Big Bang, we are told, there was a period of 300,000 years until the temperature of the original fireball dropped to 3000 degrees, when it became cool enough for electrons to combine with protons and form atoms. The process of differentiation brought a new opportunity; a new 'day' had dawned.

*

And God said:
  'Let there be a dome in the midst of the waters, and let
  it separate the waters from the waters.'
So God made the dome and separated the waters that
were under the dome from the waters that were above the
dome. And it was so. God called the dome Sky. And there
was evening and there was morning, the second day.

Genesis 1:3–5

The second day brings a second distinction. It speaks to us of the controlled security of our existence under God's providence. The borders of chaos are pushed back; the threatening waters are given their specific boundaries. A 'dome' or 'vault' or 'firmament' is provided. Some kind of solidity is inserted into the amorphous and undifferentiated mass of matter. Without this distinction, nothing further could develop. It represents the difference in solidity between the three states of matter: gases, liquids and solids. Only because these states are flexible, distinct from each other yet able to be changed into each other, is it possible for development to take place. We have an environment which combines permanence and change, not too absolutely hot and not too absolutely cold. We are approaching the possibility of the formation of planet earth. The sun is far too hot for anything to stay put, and the moon is too cold for anything to alter. But earth gives the opportunity for the development of organic compounds, and of rational minds to observe them.

*

And God said,
'Let the waters under the sky be gathered together into one place, and let the dry land appear.'
And it was so. God called the dry land Earth, and the waters that were gathered together he called Seas. And God saw that it was good. Then God said,
'Let the earth put forth vegetation; plants yielding seed, and fruit trees of every kind on earth that bear fruit with the seed in it.'
And it was so. The earth brought forth vegetation; plants yielding seed of every kind, and trees of every kind bearing fruit with the seed in it. And God saw that it was

good. And there was evening and there was morning, the third day.

Genesis 1:9–13

So God is developing the creation by making boundaries. One of the most intense human fears is the fear of being drowned, of being overwhelmed by uncontrollable water. God gives water its due location. He makes an environment which can be trusted. He does not, at this stage, create anything new; but he develops new ways of organizing what already is. This is most clearly the case with the formation of the earth. The continents take shape. An area of security for air-breathing creatures is provided. It has a definable surface, on which creatures can learn to move. Above is the vault of heaven, the sky which overarches us and contains us. It speaks to us of our boundaries, our horizons beyond which we cannot see.

So earth and water and air have been separated and distinguished. These, along with light, are the necessities for life to emerge. The earth is spoken of as 'mother' – she 'brings forth' all manner of children from her womb. The first creatures to be born of earth are, according to Genesis, plants and fruit-trees. The characteristic feature of vegetable life is its concern for the future. It is a machine for reproducing itself. Its inspirational mechanism is 'the selfish gene'. It has its constant cycles of germination, growth and seeding. The plants do not move themselves across space, so they are not considered to have 'life' in the same way as animals, but they can and do move themselves across time. They also diversify into millions of different forms. They stay in their orders. They are a sign of reliability. The apparent difference between seeds may be very slight, but the range of different kinds of plant and tree is immense.

Jesus may have been a carpenter by trade, but, to judge from his teaching, he was a gardener by inclination. Parables from this sector of creation were evidently much more interesting to him than any which could be drawn from the apparently more exciting world of animals. He noted the progress from invisibility to visibility in the progress from seed to plant; he recognized the instinctive ability of plants to overcome hazards, and the sheer increase of size in their life-cycle; he commented on the role of plant-life in indicating and responding to the changes of the seasons. And he drew attention to both the continuity and the discontinuity between the seed which is cast into the earth and apparently wasted, and the resulting plant, which emerges as a new level of existence. Resurrection is not a matter of collecting the old stuff and giving it another lease of life. It is a move into a new structure of existence, in which the old is not wasted but is transformed. This most specific image of the final goal and destiny of human life is taken from a simple observation of botanical life, which, in the understanding of Genesis, is the first sign of movement in the world.[5]

For Reflection

A few miles south of Wrexham, there is a road, the B5434, running between the A539 at Trevor and the A5 at Froncysyllte. Halfway along, at the old bridge across the River Dee, there is a minor road running west. This road follows the Dee for about a quarter of a mile. At first, there are lots of rocks in the river. The water is usually turbulent and very busy-looking. Then, round the corner, there is a very deep, wide pool, so deep as to be really dangerous. I have twice seen this pool completely frozen over, for many days on end. If you find this pool, or something similar, stop and consider it. The busy, rocky area of the river does not freeze; in contrast, the surface of the pool can appear dead and motionless. But it is in the darkness of the pool that the fish will be happily going about their business.

Questions for Working Groups

1. Leaving aside your religious commitment, how far do you actually feel that there is one good God in authority over everything? Does the world look as if that is true, in your experience?

2. Have you seen something creative happening in a situation of chaos?

3. Later in this book, in Chapter 4, we will note that there is rather a shortage of Christian hymns celebrating God as Creator. Could you start to look around for good hymns and songs on this theme? There are several in the first section of Volume 1 of the Iona Community's *Wild Goose Songs* (Glasgow, 1987); you might find them helpful as inspiration in your prayers together.

2

Creating Life

And God said,
  'Let there be lights in the dome of the sky to separate
  the day from the night; and let them be for signs and
  for seasons and for days and for years, and let them be
  lights in the dome of the sky to give light upon the
  earth.'
And it was so. God made the two great lights – the
greater light to rule the day and the lesser light to rule the
night – and the stars. God set them in the dome of the sky
to give light upon the earth, to rule over the day and over
the night, and to separate the light from the darkness.
And God saw that it was good. And there was evening
and there was morning, the fourth day.

Genesis 1:14–19

In the middle of the creation of living things, we hear about
the creation of sun and moon and stars. This is obviously
wrong. It does not require a modern scientific world-view
to tell us that the sun must have come into being before
there could be flowers on earth. Our dependence on the sun
is a very ancient wisdom.

This is the most obvious point where the main theological purpose of our authors shines through. If, against the

most elementary observation, Genesis sandwiches the creation of the sun between the creation of carrots and of codfish, there must be a good reason.

Genesis is emphasizing as sharply as possible that the sun and moon and stars are lumps of the created order along with carrots and codfish, no less and certainly no more. In biblical times, as in our own day, there has never been a shortage of people who have wanted to claim some special magical character for the lights of the sky. For most of the time when people have studied the stars, this study has been based on the understanding that the stars govern or reveal the destiny of nations or of individuals. This was certainly true of the culture under which the Hebrew people were being oppressed in their exile in Babylon at the time when this part of Genesis was being formed. The authors are delivering a fundamental attack on the fatalistic world-view held by the powerful overlords of their day; they are insisting that the sun and moon and stars are physical things, part of the good creation of the one true God, the God who is known to the exiled community but not to the oppressors.

In making a statement that is scientifically wrong, our authors are making a statement that is theologically right. Not only this, they are actually striking a blow for the liberation of the human mind which can make scientific study possible. For us to be able to study natural objects, we have to be freed from the constraints of religious presuppositions; we have to be free from the notion that some natural objects are, in their own nature, somehow supernatural, or magical or enchanted. The Hebrew mind, at this point, is making a profoundly religious statement, to give a non-religious status to the most obviously powerful objects of nature. God is the one authority, under whom all people live. It is God's hand which creates, and God does not yield his authority to any inanimate object. The stars are part of creation; they are part of the same programme as the rest of us. Indeed, we are of the same stuff as they are. Every atom of carbon in every living being was once inside a star, and we are made out of the ashes of stars which are no more.[1] My own future, my work and my relationships, are not governed by mindless things far away; nor are they subject to anonymous forces such as 'fate'.

At the beginning of the gospel of Christ, according to Matthew, we have a similar message. Eastern astrologers, practitioners of the secret fatalistic science of the Babylonians, find their way to the infant Christ and hand over gifts which represent the tools of their trade. The early Christian teacher, Ignatius of Antioch, saw this as a death-blow to superstition, an end to the power of sorcery.[2] But still, many people in our modern world feel that they are not truly free, that they are victims, that they are controlled by some mindless fate, some impersonal force which makes words such as 'freedom', 'guilt' or 'responsibility' seem to be empty pretences. What they call this sort of force does not matter very much; it can be heredity, environment, the market, conditioning, or 'the system'. The Christian movement is called to insist that all these powers are not autonomous, rather, that they are responsible to their Maker. We human beings are to be defined not so much by the features which are unalterably determined but by our ability to respond to the unpredictable, to the unknown, to the love of God and the love of our neighbour.

The lights of heaven do not govern the wills and choices of human beings. But they are not without authority: they rule the day and the night. People make all sorts of other measurements which vary according to culture and language; we may talk of ounces or kilograms, miles or stadia, escudos or francs, quarts or litres. The one form of measurement which is universal is that of time, which comes not from invention but from experience. It comes from outside our separate cultures. Perhaps not everyone bothers about seconds or minutes or weeks, but days and months and years have an authority which all people acknowledge. Modern city-life may try to abolish the night; the effect is that many literate modern people have a poorer knowledge of the stars than our peasant ancestors did. The darkness of the night-sky is so polluted by street-lights and floodlights – yes, including the floodlights of churches! – that modern people know the stars more through books than by actually seeing them. A lot of electricity is wasted by poorly aimed floodlighting; the effect is a haze of light around the lower 20 degrees or so of the night sky, which affects visibility even in rural areas. We hear even of a project of macho technology, that we might be better able to control the seasons on earth if we destroyed the moon.[3] If we go any way down that sort of road, we shall be inviting the natural order to take revenge on the human species, the most destructive pests on earth.

In spite of such fantasies of non-dependence, the language of evening and morning remains with us, and has been with us from the beginning. Sun and moon have a function which puts all people under their authority. But it is a mindless authority, a limited role. We surrender our rights if we allow ourselves to be persuaded that they have any greater authority. However fascinating the comet may be, however magnificent the star may be, the poorest child is more significant. The child can know something of the star, but the star can know nothing of the child. 'Sun and moon and stars may be above your physical body, but they are beneath your soul... There is nothing higher than yourself in the natural order, save God alone.'[4]

*

And God said,
    'Let the waters bring forth swarms of living creatures,
    and let birds fly above the earth across the dome of the
    sky.'
So God created the great sea monsters and every living
creature that moves, of every kind, with which the waters
swarm, and every winged bird of every kind. And God
saw that it was good. God blessed them, saying,
    'Be fruitful and multiply and fill the waters in the seas,
    and let birds multiply on the earth.'
And there was evening and there was morning, the fifth
day.

                                                    Genesis 1:20–23

Creation, according to this first chapter of Genesis, is a
process of phases which are linked together in continuity.
But there are moments when something irreversibly new
occurs; these are marked by the verb 'create' – a word
whose root meaning in Hebrew is to 'cut'. God 'creates' the
heavens and the earth; he 'makes' the firmament or dome,
and the lights; he 'makes' mineral and vegetable things. But
with birds and fish there is a new start. God 'creates' living
things. Birds and fish are like plants in that they reproduce
according to their species. But they are seen as really living
things; they can move around; their reproduction appears
to be less automatic. They can respond to commands, and
so God speaks to them. They are called 'living beings'; the
same word is used to describe them as is used in chapter 2,
verse 7, to describe the creation of the human being, the
word which the old versions translate as 'a living soul'.

   The more we look around, even just at the other planets
in the solar system, the more clear it becomes that the
arrival of life has been an extraordinarily finely adjusted

process. Scientific writers seem to have an inexhaustible list of the coincidences which have been required in order that life could emerge. 'If the electric charge of the electron had been only slightly different, stars would either have been unable to burn hydrogen and helium, or else they would not have exploded.'[5] Or, if, in the initial explosion which set off the formation of the universe, the matching of explosive vigour to gravitating power had been ever so slightly less accurate, nothing, including the processes of life, would have been able to get going. The degree of accuracy required was the same as if one were to fire a bullet to hit a one-inch target on the other side of the observable universe, twenty billion light-years away.[6]

The authors of Genesis do not try to identify the very beginnings of life on earth. They have no knowledge of what we would call the 'pre-historic', of fossils or of bacteria. It is sufficient for them that there was a beginning of life, a unique event. The result is a sky full of birds and a sea full of fish. The living creatures that are least like ourselves come on the scene first. This process is very different to the understanding of nature which we find in some other religious world-views, which speak of nature going round and round in ceaseless repetition. The picture in Genesis is more appropriate to the teachings of modern biology. There is a hierarchy in the development of life. The more complex follows on from the less complex. Evolutionary events are unpredictable, and largely unrepeatable.

Life first appears in the water. It is not clear whether biological science can draw a precise border-line between the non-living and the living. Our authors are not concerned about the border-lines; they are concerned about the clear fact that there is a vast difference between non-living things as a whole and living things as a whole. And so, instead of starting off with an account of tiny organisms such as bacteria, they introduce us first to the huge creatures whose ability to move themselves around is absurdly obvious. Sea-monsters are scary. They are at home in an element which is threatening and fearsome to us, where all is dark and there are no landmarks. The sea-monster is that hidden shapeless thing which jumps out at us from the immemorial past. Such monsters are not far away from our social and personal imaginations. Genesis is saying that even these creatures are part of the good creation. They are under God's authority, even though they live in the realms of darkness and chaos.

The author of Revelation tells of the demonic power of a sea-monster which comes up on the land and attracts worship from the people of the world. This is a surrender to the things of darkness, to hidden threats which creep out and claim a false and corrupting honour for themselves. Christ is the master of the monster when it is given recognition and status beyond its right. Christ is the victor even in that wayward area of our human nature, our imagination.

The creatures come into existence according to their species. Our authors do not know about an evolutionary process by which this happens. They do not know about such creatures as dinosaurs, which existed long before there were humans to observe them. They do know about the evolutionary descendents of the dinosaurs, the birds; they do know about the astonishing variety of ways in which a bird can be a bird. They know that birds can overcome the hazards that threaten them, and that therefore birds can multiply. Perhaps they can also recognize the extra potential that seems to be built into birds – the extra sense which some birds have but which modern humans don't have, to identify the earth's magnetic field and to steer by it; or the extra potential of agility which seems to be built into birds, which gives them the ability to avoid metal vehicles moving at 70 miles per hour, an ability which can never have been required of them until recent generations. This is all part of the response to the mandate 'Be fruitful and multiply'. The practical mandate is not 'survive by being the fittest'; if that were the case, only a few species would survive. The mandate that such creatures follow is 'survive by being adaptable'. And that is true not only for birds.

God blesses these creatures. They are worth being, in their own right. They do not have to be useful or interesting to humans. A few years ago, some naturalists found an unusually highly-coloured bird, which had never before been seen by people, in a forest in Papua New Guinea; someone commented that it was wasted there because no one could see it. As far as the bird itself was concerned, it was no more interesting and no less interesting than a crow. That would surely be the Creator's valuation. The crow is as worthy of God's blessing as any other bird, however glamorous in human eyes. But there is a new danger for many species now; their failure to survive will not be because of lack of fitness, but because they are not sufficiently interesting to human beings. It is possible that, if 'progress' continues as it has been, whole areas could be depopulated of natural fauna, and only the animals that humans have domesticated or protected will survive.

❋

And God said,
   'Let the earth bring forth living creatures of every
   kind: cattle and creeping things and wild animals of
   the earth of every kind.'
And it was so. God made the wild animals of the earth of
every kind, and the cattle of every kind, and everything
that creeps upon the ground of every kind. And God saw
that it was good.

Genesis 1:24–25

So we come to the sixth day. We are on dry land. We are home. The creatures that earth brings forth are those which we know most closely. Cattle come first. For millions of people, life without cattle would not be life. Cattle are wealth, status, security. Next on the list come ants and bugs and cockroaches. Whether we like it or not, life would not be recognizable as normal life if these companions were absent. They scurry around, taking little notice of us. We crush them underfoot, feeling slightly guilty, perhaps, because we know that they were here first.

The creatures appear according to their species. This emphasizes the regularity of nature: if two sheep mate they do not produce a giraffe. But it also affirms nature's freedom to be various. Creatures grow in company with other creatures. They adapt themselves to each other's presence – sorting out the question of who eats whom, but also finding ways in which they are of mutual advantage to each other.

God looks at this part of creation, in all its variety, with all its potential for destructiveness and pain. He sees that it is 'good'. It is good that creatures have to try to solve the problems of their conditions of existence, for these enable them to become what they are. It is good that species can develop, and that mutations can occur; and, if this is so, it is good, not only that a bat can develop from a mouse, but that a nasty parasite can develop from a nice free-swimming crustacean; not only that a musical genius can be born of stupid parents but that a deaf child can be born of hearing parents; not only that the law of gravity keeps things reliably in place, but also that it will operate to bring an aircraft hurtling to earth if its engines fail.

Taking creation as a whole, we may find much to regret; we may want to accuse the Creator of having made a cruelly bad job of it. But if we ask, 'How can God allow this to happen?', let us ask conscientiously, 'What other kind of world would you prefer? What sort of world would it be where such uncongenial developments were impossible?' It would have to be a world where the laws of nature were unreliable, where the rain fell only on the just and not on the unjust; and this would be a kind of bribery. It would have to be a world in which, in order to avoid the possibility of uncongenial development or mutation, no development or mutation at all would be possible; there would have to be exact reproduction from parent to offspring. A few species do seem to have got stuck like this; but do we envy them? Parents who (like myself) have children who are classed as 'disabled' recognize that the disability is part of the risk of being in a world of development and genetic hazards. God could have made a ready-made world, fixed and complete in itself. But, in fact, he seems to have chosen to make a creation which is in the process of making itself. It is a world with some false starts and blind alleys, so it seems; some types emerge which are fruitful and some not. But the Spirit is within; God is at work inside the mysterious haphazardness of the world. We accept the joys and fascination of such a world, along with its risks and pains. There is, certainly, something that we can call evil, and the book of Genesis as a whole does not pretend otherwise; we shall come to this in due course. But at this point, our authors are asking us to face the demand of believing in a good Creator. In effect, they ask us, 'Which would you prefer to be – a person as you are, afraid of getting cancer or having a handicapped child, hoping for the vision of God or true love with another person different from yourself, alarmed and encouraged by the differences between yourself and your parents, *or* a unicellular citizen tucked away in a unicellular bed?' You can't have it both ways. The fact remains that this is the world that you have got, and that you will not do much good either to yourself or to the rest of the world if your remarks always start with 'if only ...' If only fire didn't burn ... But fire does burn. That is what is.

At what is, God looks; and he sees that it is good.

God knows what he sees and speaks of what he knows. He keeps on saying that what he has made is good. He both makes and loves his creation. This is the example for all those who work and who produce; but many people do not have the opportunity to love what they make, or to be enthusiastic about it. The most important human creative work is, surely, in the bearing and upbringing of our children. If we are to be good at this, we probably need to get into practice with making and loving simpler and less demanding things first. We need to find ways, which are realistic and not merely sentimental, of affirming the lovableness of what is around us. From a fairly early age, many children will get the message that they are not really lovable, that they are not really valued, that they are problems rather than assets in society. They will start to act in accordance with their unlovedness. The Christian gospel states that the supreme truth about us is that we are loved by our Creator, that nothing can separate us from this love, and that we do not have to earn it in competition with others. This builds on the statement at the beginning of the Bible that God saw what he had made, and it was good. Christians can go further, and state that the supreme moment where the Word of God asserts that all is very good is when Christ himself looks at his own work on the cross, and announces 'It is finished.' The new creation starts at the supreme point of chaos and darkness and the combined effectiveness of the forces of evil. The followers of Christ may find their own discovery of goodness similarly, at the point where evil seems to be doing its worst.

For Reflection

Try to find a place where the night-sky is not too badly spoiled by light pollution – somewhere like the middle of an area of moorland, the shores of Llyn Clywedog, or even on a North Sea ferry! Rest your eyes in the stars. Think about their distance from you: you are not seeing them as they are, you are seeing them as they were when their light started on its journey to you – that would be four years ago, in the case of the nearest star, thousands or millions of years ago, in the case of more distant ones. In some cases, the light you see is coming to you from stars which have been dead for ages – it's as if you could hear now the voices of Julius Caesar or Moses or the Buddha. That says something about the size of creation.

> Now all the heavenly splendour
> Breaks forth in starlight tender
> From myriad worlds unknown;
> And man, the marvel seeing,
> Forgets his selfish being,
> For joy of beauty not his own.[7]

Questions for Working Groups

1. Harvest Festivals seem to be more and more concerned with decoration, with picking out the pretty things of creation, and not with the whole range. Harvest is about human work, working with the rest of creation to create wealth. How are you going to celebrate Harvest this year?

2. Do you think that people nowadays feel themselves to be victims of mindless fate – whether astrological or economic or whatever? How do you work out a gospel response?

3

Creating Us

Then God said,
> *'Let us make humankind in our image, according to our likeness; and let them have dominion over the fish of the sea, and over the birds of the air, and over the cattle, and over all the wild animals of the earth, and over every creeping thing that creeps upon the earth.'*
So God created humankind in his image, in the image of God he created them; male and female he created them. God blessed them, and God said to them,
> *'Be fruitful and multiply, and fill the earth and subdue it; and have dominion over the fish of the sea and over the birds of the air and over every living thing that moves upon the earth.'*

Genesis 1:26–28

So far, God's word has been, 'Let there be ...' Now there seems to be a pause. God stops and reflects. God says to Godself, 'Let us make ...' God speaks of making a being in God's own image. This must mean, among other things, that the new creature will be one who can reflect and plan, as God can. Indeed, the new creature will be one which can look at what has been made and learn from it, as God can. God learns by seeing how the creation works, in all its variety and unpredictable interactions. The human being is created to be an artist, like God.

God says to Godself, 'Let *us* make ...' God is somehow plural. God's mind is able to hold a conversation with itself. Christian teachers have seen this as a foreshadowing of the belief in the Trinity, the multiple character of God's nature. God is a community of love even before there is any creation to be loved. God is love. In the divine nature, at the heart of the universe, the principle of power is subservient to the principle of love. God clears space for a new creature who will be like God, and that new creature is us.

So, from the start, both God and human are plural. This is part of what it means for us to be made in the image and likeness of God. The most basic factor in this plurality is the factor of sex. Male on his own and female on her own are not properly the image of God, because God is both. God needs both female and male in order to provide an image of Godself. Like many other writers, I struggle with the problem of what pronoun to use in referring to God. I could put 'he' in quotes all the time, to show that I don't really mean the masculine pronoun. Alternatively, I could use 'He' or '*he*' or (he) or 's/he'. I could alternate between 'he' and 'she', or I could do my best to avoid having to use pronouns at all. I settle for the traditional 'he' very reluctantly, knowing that it is bound up with all sorts of meanings and implications which I do not intend. In writing about 'God' at all, I have to fall back on G.K. Chesterton's comment: that if a thing is worth doing it's worth doing badly – a standpoint that the theologians call justification by faith.

There is no new day for this new creation. Humanity is made towards knocking-off time on the sixth day, after the making of all the mammals and reptiles. We are not separate from the rest of the animal creation. Like all other living creatures, we have emerged out of the non-living world of water, air and rocks. Like all other living creatures, we use a common mechanism for storing and using energy. In terms of our DNA inheritance, the differences between ourselves and chimpanzees are tiny; they are not much bigger between ourselves and mice. But these slight differences are critical. The authors of Genesis tell us that we are made in the same production-batch as the other mammals. But they also tell us that we are *created*; in other words, in the arrival of the humans there was a fundamental new stage. When the human is born, there is a leap from instinct to thought. This is a gigantic leap, in spite of the insignificance of the leap in anatomical terms. As with the arrival of other species, we are the result of modifications made to material which was already there. But also, there is something new, something which cannot be explained merely in terms of what went before us.

God has made all creatures. But only the humans are said to be in God's image and likeness. This must mean that humans are made to be creators. They take what is already there, and create from it something that has never been before. This has to be true in the most universal type of human creativity, in the relationship between our parents and ourselves, and between ourselves and our children. It is also true in our use of things to make other things. 'In a normal society, one, that is to say, composed of persons who are responsible for what they do and what they make, the artist is not a special kind of man, but every man is a special kind of artist.'[1] This was a favourite remark of Eric Gill; he was not only a sculptor and graphic artist, he was also a designer of printed and carved letters, and many of today's ordinary printed pages are evidence of his art. The trouble is that, for most of us, our imagination and our artistic abilities are encouraged a lot at the beginning of our education, and then less and less as we grow older – unless we go in for the sort of 'art' that makes us special and cuts us off from the rest of humanity. (I have sometimes suggested that teachers ought to be paid according to the amount of the pupil's total personality that they take responsibility for educating – imagination, relationships, emotions, as well as intellect; on that showing, infant teachers would get ten times the pay of university professors.)

We can speak of God as Creator because as human beings we know something about being creators ourselves. The same Spirit of God who was active at the beginning of creation is also at work in an artist such as Bezalel, son of Uri, master craftsman.[2] Our experience of being creators can give us language for thinking about God. Some artists and dramatists see this more clearly than many of the professional theologians. One who did so was Dorothy L. Sayers, who was primarily a novelist and playwright; it is a pity that her insight has not been more widely recognized in theological circles. She expressed her teaching most succinctly in a speech put into the mouth of the Archangel Michael at the end of her play *The Zeal of Thy House*. She sees the work of creation as a threefold structure: the basic and originating idea or purpose of the work; the hard practical work, using energy in time and space; and the power or presence or effect of the work as it is recognized by other people. Each of these is the creation; each is essential to the creation; and if one or other is weak or ineffective, the whole creation is flawed. That is the analysis of an artist, and anyone who has tried to paint, compose or write anything will see that it is valid. Sayers claims that this is a mirror of God as God is disclosed in the central Christian doctrine of the Trinity; she maintains that it reflects the unity-in-diversity of God, Father, Son and Spirit. I find this an illuminating and fruitful approach, which leads into other similar links and analogies. More than any other account of the doctrine of the Trinity, it connects with the human experience of making things. It connects with the vision of human beings in Genesis, that we are made to be makers, and, when we make, we can see our activity as a mirroring of the creative character of God.[3] We do not have

to be into the artistic stratosphere for this approach to
make sense. It speaks to me as someone who was trained to
repair aeroplanes; it can also speak to gardeners and cooks.
As Eric Gill maintained, 'Everyone is a special kind of
artist.'

God is free to create. Human beings, made in the image
of God, are made with this freedom. God is free, because he
has chosen his creative work, in continuing it and sustain-
ing it. God's freedom is not the freedom of being constantly able to choose. Freedom of choice can become a deceptive
nonsense. In our modern consumer society, for example,
we are provided with vast ranges of almost identical
vehicles and prepacked chicken curry and television games.
We maintain maximum consumption and expenditure of
fuel, as huge trucks trundle past each other carrying bottles
of water, some from Scotland to France and some from
France to Scotland – all in the name of freedom of choice.
Freedom to choose can be a block, a standstill. The driver
who has to choose between two roads knows this; so does
the woman who has to choose between two men. We are
free when we *have chosen*. Then we can move, and create,
like God. God is free because, although we know him as
Trinity, he also is undivided. God wills what he knows and
loves. God knows what he wills and loves. God loves what
he wills and knows. God is not free because he can choose
between good and evil; rather, God is free because he has
chosen. We are free when we have chosen. But, more profoundly still, we are free when we *have been chosen* – the
man and woman who have committed themselves to each
other in marriage know this. We are made in the image and
likeness of God. We have been chosen. God's service is perfect freedom.

We are trusted images. We need to learn to trust our
own image-making ability. Again, our experience, often
as children, tells us the opposite. We are told that our

language, our way of seeing things, will not fit or is not normal. Profoundly deaf children, whose 'native' or natural communication is with visual signs, find themselves forced to fit into a world of hearing and of speech, where they are always going to be second-class citizens.[4] Many children have been told so often that they can't sing that they grow up believing it – until they meet someone like John Bell of the Iona Community, who is able to undo the damage.[5] The word of the powerful to people who are deaf or disabled can be summed up as 'You can't but I can'; so, let me do it for you. We might assume that the 'human being' who is made in the image of God is some sort of ideal person, a super athlete or dancer or singer, or someone who can represent all that is most splendid and perfect. Can the 'image of God' be deaf or disabled, stupid or illiterate? The authors of Genesis knew what they were writing about. When they wrote about cattle or reptiles, they were writing about cattle and reptiles as they knew them, not about some idealized cattle and reptiles in a long-past golden age. So when they wrote about human beings, they were writing about human beings as they knew them. What they knew was not a peaceful, successful, dominant section of humanity, riding high in civic and moral superiority. They knew exile and enslavement; they knew the massive propensity for things to go wrong, and for the powerful members of the human race to treat the less powerful as rubbish. In a profoundly divided and cruel world, they raised the astonishing chorus, 'We are made in the image of God.' This is our story, this is our song. Those who make this claim difficult to believe are not the disabled, the enslaved or the stupid; the ones who cause the problem are those who try to perch themselves high above the common human race, and who think that they have all the answers. Even the Church can find itself becoming an organization for congratulating the powerful on being powerful.

According to Paul, Christ is the image of the invisible God. In Christ, God is recognizable. But this is because, in Christ, the divine nature is both hidden and displayed.[6] Christ had the human likeness of a slave. We can accept this only if we let Christ re-define what we mean by 'God'. Christ shows us the image of God stripped of dignity and splendour. In turn, we can accept this message of the creation story only if we are willing to accept our fellow human beings in terms of that which is hidden, not in terms of that which is outwardly verifiable, impressive and successful. The image of God, for us, is the man hanging in darkness on a cross.

God makes the human beings male and female. God does not start by making an individual but a partnership. They start off together. God invents human sexuality. The authors were perfectly well aware of the difference between cows and bulls, but they do not draw attention to this difference in their account of the making of cattle. In the case of humans, it is necessary for the point to be made. It is too easy for one of the partners to be seen as the normal and the other to be a kind of accessory. Moreover, it is also too easy for sexuality itself to be devalued and seen as something which has got nothing to do with God. But our sexual method of reproduction is the guarantor of biological variety and individual uniqueness. The potential of this mechanism means that the number of possible genotypes is vastly greater than the number of atoms in the entire universe. Every human being is the carrier of a unique genotype. Sexual reproduction is a creative process; it enables biological novelty.[7]

So there is a profoundly significant statement of the classification of human beings. But then, there is an equally significant silence. At other phases of creation, the authors have been keen to draw attention to the various types of creature, according to their kinds. So we might expect that this emphasis on classification would come to its climax in the human creation. But there is nothing here about Semitic or Negroid or Caucasian humans, nothing about Israelite or Hindu or Buddhist humans, nothing about introvert or extrovert humans. The adjectives by which we distinguish various kinds of people are notably absent. The emphasis is on the unity of the human race, made in the image of the one God. And we need to note again that the authors of Genesis did not write in ignorance of racial divisions. Their nation had been experiencing a deep corporate suffering caused by their oppression at the hands of another national group. In fact, this experience did lead to a sharpening of Jewish national self-awareness. So it is all the more remarkable that there is no trace of racial consciousness in this account of creation. They had, indeed, shared in a terrible experience. But they did not allow that experience to be their only truth. Human beings do not simply learn from experience. They learn by reflecting on experience, and sometimes by defying experience. Experience, taken simply, will tell us that the sun goes round the earth; it tells many people that black people are inferior to white people, that deaf people are stupid, that females are designed to be subservient to males. Experience gives us what we know as common sense knowledge; and common sense, according to Einstein, is the name we give to the accumulation of prejudices laid down before the age of 18.

God speaks, as he has done to other creatures: be fruitful, and multiply, and fill the earth. The command to multiply is given to adults. Of course it does mean: bear children. But it also means: produce responsible adults. It is a mandate to the whole of society to enable infants to grow up and to become mature. All sorts of institutions – of education, public health, politics, local government, finance, commerce, the arts, as well as religion and the family – receive their blessing and their commissioning.

The human beings are told to fill the earth and to 'rule' it – to take responsibility for it. We can fill the earth, in the sense that we are so adaptable that we can make some sort of dwelling-place for ourselves in almost all the climates of the planet. The only animal which is as ubiquitous as ourselves, in its natural state, is the rat. Although our genetic inheritance is so similar to that of some other species, we have the one extraordinary advantage. Our big brain is the most complex thing in the whole physical creation. As some birds seem to have a greater agility than they have needed for survival, until they started to have to avoid motor cars, so we humans have a far greater brain-power than is necessary for survival. No one *has* to understand the equations of higher mathematics in order to survive! The most extraordinary thing in physics is the brain of the physicist – which is not different to the brain of either the early human hunter-gatherers or the modern slave-workers in cocoa plantations. While other creatures have specialized in all sorts of other ways, with big teeth, and shells, and wings, we humans have remained comparatively feeble and defenceless, except for this one great asset. T. H. White spells this out in his story of how God created all the embryos of all the creatures (which, at the embryo stage, all look more or less alike), and gave them all the chance to develop their own specialized equipment. One embryo refused the offer and insisted on staying as it was. God was greatly pleased and called up the others.

Here, all you embryos, come here with your beaks and what-nots to look upon our first man. He is the only one of you who has guessed Our riddle, out of all of you, and we have great pleasure in conferring upon him the Order of Dominion over the Fowls of the Air, and the Beasts of the Earth, and the Fishes of the Sea. Now the rest of you, get along, and love and multiply, for it is time to knock

off for the weekend. As for you, Man, you will be a
naked tool all your life, though a user of tools; you will
look like an embryo until they bury you, but all others
will be embryos before your might; eternally undevel-
oped, you will always remain potentially in Our image.[8]

God does not say much about things which the humans
are to possess. He tells them about things which they are
going to do. Verbs, rather than nouns, are in God's commands. God does not make a great song about the big
brain, with its hundred thousand million neurons, that we
are being blessed with. He does not tell us that we are being
given minds. But we are going to be able to fulfil functions,
to do jobs. This, I suggest, is a helpful way of speaking.
Philosophers and scientists have spent much energy in trying to sort out the relationship between mind and brain, as
if mind is one thing and brain is another thing. But this is
partly a matter of the words we use. The English language
tells us that there is a thing called a mind, and that a mind
is a thing which we possess. 'Mind' is a noun; and the verb
'to mind' is about something quite different. Zulu has no
separate noun for 'mind'; if I want to refer to my mind, I
speak of my 'ukucabanga', and 'ukucabanga' is simply the
infinitive form of the verb 'to think'.[9] So, I don't have a
'mind' at all. I do something; I think. My mind is me, thinking. Similarly, my body is me, bodying. And my soul is me,
souling. Personally, I find that this is not only a relaxing
way of thinking, but one that is seriously true.

What God gives is a mandate and an ability to act, in
his image. We are told to look after the rest of creation, to
take responsibility for it, to keep it in order. This does
mean using power; it means taking political responsibility.
Our use of power is part of our response to God's call and
blessing; and we remember that the authors of this chapter
had plenty of experience of the ways in which the use of

political power can go wrong. But it is vital that we notice to whom God gives this power: it is to the human partnership as a whole, not to a privileged few. Any system which deprives healthy and adult people of an opportunity to exercise power is failing to fulfil God's mandate. Good people sometimes look at the ways in which power is misused and feel that it is impossible to reconcile such power with the command to love; but the chances are that they will be missing out on the opportunity to correct injustice and to show love to many who most need it.

Traditional translations use the words 'dominion' and 'rule' at this point; these have been understood as giving us the right to do as we like with the rest of creation, to exploit it, to use it as a plaything, to take it as a source of weapons with which to destroy each other or compete with each other. 'Dominion' has been understood as meaning 'domination' – domination of the environment, and the use of things of the environment as means for dominating people. So, vast herds of bison are shot for fun; animals are hunted not for food but for 'sport'. Some people – men especially – seem to pride themselves on the amount of power that they employ; it seems to me that a man who requires 200 horsepower to shift him around must be very weak, compared to someone who needs only 60. And the largest human creations in earth and water and sky are dustbowls, polluted waters and smog.

Other translations use the phrase 'I am putting you in charge ...' This is a helpful way of expressing the meaning of God's mandate to us. It is true to the general witness of Scripture. If God 'puts us in charge', this means that we are caretakers for God; we are accountable to God for the earth's condition. God's voice is represented by our grandchildren, who have every right to ask us, 'What kind of condition is the earth going to be in when we grow up? Please leave it in the condition in which you would like to find it.'

We are given responsibility for how the land and its fruitfulness are used. A good clean field of wheat represents centuries of human interference in nature. This is success, and we may see it as a proper fulfilling of our mandate. How far does this go? There is legitimate debate about the use of genetically modified seeds. In one sense, this is simply continuing the tradition of producing more fertile types of seed.[10] But if it leads to the use of sterile 'terminator' seed, which does not produce a plant whose seeds can be used for sowing for the next crop, then great new power is being taken by the seed companies, and this can put farmers, especially farmers in the poorest areas of the world, into new and inescapable dependency. Even in Britain, small farmers have had to accept the advice that fertilizer and pesticide firms give concerning their own product; larger farmers have been able to save money by paying for independent advice. There are real questions which require the skill and competence of botanists and chemists; there are others which involve economic justice.

God remains God; nothing in this part of the story can obscure the great central statement of the Bible: 'The earth is the Lord's, and all that is in it: the world and its people belong to the Lord.' There is all the difference in the world between ownership and stewardship. This vision of God's claim upon the whole of humanity came to a people who had known, only too well, the harshness of being under another nation's 'dominion'. 'The earth is the Lord's' is the song of people who had been slaves, and who knew that a practical conviction of this kind had to be cherished and celebrated, if they were going to avoid falling into slavery again. Slavery happens when one group exercises total dominion over another, and prevents them from having any responsibility for or reward from the work which they perform. According to the International Labour Organization, more than 250 million children were working in slave-

labour conditions in 1997. As one such worker said on a
TV documentary in 2000, 'If you eat this chocolate, you are
eating my flesh.' There are more slaves in the world today
than ever before. This is one of the most powerful motives
for supporting fair trade organizations, which guarantee
that the products which we purchase are produced by
workers who are paid fair wages. When whole nations are
trapped in unpayable debts, so that most of the value of
their work goes into paying the debt rather than into
improving their own basic living conditions, this is rightly
seen as a new form of slavery. The millennium is celebrated
as a jubilee year; and jubilee means, deep down, not just a
reinstatement of the right of the poorest but a renewed
affirmation that the earth is the Lord's.

It is no accident that our failure to recognize the unity of
the human race goes hand in hand with the despoiling of
the rest of creation. A great deal of the waste and pollution
of the earth happens not because of ignorance or careless-
ness, but because people use things in trying to destroy
other people. War permits destruction which would otherwise not be tolerated. Companies in competition with each
other use raw materials to make more products than are
really necessary for the well-being of the human race as a
whole. We become strangers to each other, and we become
unfriendly towards the earth. Prosperity brings more buying-
power; more goods are demanded; more journeys have to
be made in order to deliver them. We are coming to the
point where we measure a nation's economic success by
how far its traffic is gridlocked.

From outer space, no national boundaries can be seen,
and there is certainly no evidence that some areas are
Catholic or Protestant or Orthodox. But our attitude to the
land itself is the most basic way in which we fail to recognize that the earth is the Lord's. We carve the land up into
portions and we say, 'This is mine, and not yours'; 'Private

– keep out'. In the law of Moses, no groups and no individuals had the right to call the land their own to do what they liked with, for the land was God's alone. God had delivered them from slavery, and slavery was all part of a system which gave landrights to a few and kept the majority of the population landless and non-responsible. So any monopolizing of land was not merely injustice towards a fellow human being; it was a failure in the worship of God the Deliverer. The families of Israel were all tenants of the God of Israel. Each family had an 'inheritance' – a space for which it was responsible. On that land, they created wealth; from this wealth, they paid God an offering of the first-fruits, as a kind of token rental. And from this wealth, they ran their social security system, ensuring the well-being of the orphan, the widow, and the unregistered alien.[11] There was one tribe which did not have an area of land allocated to it. This was the tribe of Levi; the Levites had the special responsibility of serving the Temple, so they did not have the time and opportunity to work the land. Other tribes paid tithes, from which the Levites benefited; but this was not a 'clergy stipend', it was a compensation for their loss of landrights.

Where the basic reverence for the land is ignored, it is only too easy for people to be moved around without their consent, in order, for instance, to enable islands in the Indian Ocean to be used as airforce bases. Boundaries can be set up, as they have been in Southern and Central and West Africa, not for the benefit of the local people, not as a way of caring for the land, but as part of the hostilities and competitiveness of colonial powers. There are boundaries around Namibia that have split up traditional tribal areas just as sharply as that notorious boundary between North and South Korea. In the little town of Maple Creek, in the eastern foothills of the Canadian Rockies, there is an extraordinary museum of agricultural implements; it was created during his lifetime by a local man who, in his 80 years, spent fewer than seven nights away from home. Among other things, he had collected examples of every type of barbed wire used in that area; we counted over a 150 specimens. According to one historian, barbed wire was the single most important instrument used in the 'conquest' of the West. The Native American Chief Seattle's response to this process was prophetic:

> The white man does not understand our ways. He treats his mother, the earth, as a thing to be bought, plundered, sold like sheep or bright beads. His appetite will devour the earth and leave behind only a desert. This we know: the earth does not belong to man; man belongs to the earth. You may think that you own God as you wish to own our land; but you cannot. The earth is precious to God, and to harm the earth is to heap contempt on its Creator.[12]

In Britain we lament the loss of hedgerows, which have provided such important habitat for many kinds of wildlife. But many hedges were established for the purpose of securing private possession of land and of stopping its accessibility for the general population as common land. We wake up one day, as we did in 1998, to discover that one man can own a vast section of Snowdon, and the sum of £3,680,000 has to be raised so that a trust can buy it. It is quite a relief to know that no one owns Antarctica. Even in the more mundane scene of our domestic property, the market operates so that the value of land is set by those who have the spare money to buy it. Land values rise, and the price of properties rises, so that they are beyond the reach of people of low incomes. Unlike some other parts of the world, in Britain the value of a 'property' is expressed in a single total figure. Unless you do some fairly intricate sums, you cannot tell how much of the total value represents the value of the house and how much represents the value of the land. The cost of building, of materials and labour, has not risen much above the level of inflation over the last 20 years; it is the value of the land which has been bouncing around in such an erratic manner. Land has become merchandise. It is treated as a commodity, like furniture or vehicles. People who make commodities are entitled to sell them. But who makes land? The land is the one asset which is *given*. It is not made by people; people cannot make more of it. It is a different kind of thing to the other things which people buy and sell.

The earth is the Lord's, according to the psalm; there are many communities across the world whose traditional belief is that you can no more sell outright a piece of land than you can sell cubic yards of air. But in our modern Western societies, we have millions of people who have no real stake in the land, no real sense that they share in the wealth that is produced from the land or on the land. In a word, they are exiles. In our kind of society, it is not practicable for every family to have its own smallholding; but how do we order our land-tenure and taxation systems so that every citizen is a shareholder in the total value derived from the nation's assets? The blessing on human life here in Genesis is a word directed at people who knew only too well what it was like to be exiled. It is telling them that the claim of their Babylonian overlords is based in falsehood, that their own complacency and complicity in their fate must give way to a more positive faith. These same political issues are set before the people of our day, by the message that we are all tenants or stewards of the land. We do not have freehold rights; we are leaseholders from God, with responsibilities for maintenance and repair. Do we, in our culture, believe that the earth is the Lord's, any more than the Babylonians did? Many modern Western Christians are attracted by the spirituality of the Celts, or of Africans or of Native Americans; they seem to have had a reverence for the land, and a joy in the natural creation, which we have lost, both in our politics and in our worship. I share this enthusiasm; my concern about the land arises directly from listening to African people during the years when we lived in their continent. But we need to beware of treating the spirituality of distant peoples as yet another commodity, as something just to be interested in. Their spirituality is powerful because they saw so clearly that God was Lord of their time and place; we need to see, equally powerfully, that God is Lord not just of their time and place but of our own.

*

God said,
> 'See, I have given you every plant yielding seed that is upon the face of all the earth, and every tree with seed in its fruit; you shall have them for food. And to every beast of the earth, and to every bird of the air, and to everything that creeps on the earth, everything that has the breath of life, I have given every green plant for food.'

And it was so. God saw everything that he had made, and indeed, it was very good. And there was evening and there was morning, the sixth day.

Genesis 1:29–31

After giving to humans this responsibility to be stewards and caretakers of the rest of creation, God concludes by recognizing the inescapable fact that unites us to the rest of creation, namely, that we have to eat. Whether we are talking about cod or flies or melons, we recognize the extraordinary surplus of seed that living things produce, far more numerous than is necessary for their reproduction. The over-whelming majority of such reproductive material does not come to maturity. It is eaten. Humans take their nourish-ment alongside the beasts and the birds, with substantially the same menu.

According to this section of Genesis, there should be no need for living creatures to deprive each other of life in order to survive – this being on the authors' understanding that vegetable life is not really life at all. By the time that this chapter was written, humans were certainly carnivor-ous; the killing of animals was an essential part of the sacrificial system of worship. According to our authors, it was only after the Flood that humans were given a mandate to feed on an animal as well as a vegetable diet. So it may be only a piece of obsolescent barbarism that we eat meat. However, we clearly are not designed to be grass-eaters. It may be that the raising of beef-cattle is an inefficient and wasteful use of fertile land, and that the rapid spoliation of the South American rain-forest in order to provide cattle-land will turn out to be an unnecessary disaster. On the other hand, there are areas where the topsoil is poor and unsuitable for growing vegetables that are edible for humans. If that land can be made productive by growing herbivores on it, then perhaps we may be allowed to eat such herbivores; and so there is still place for the sheep-farmers on our hills. Even then, it is right to bear in mind the ancient connection between meat-eating and sacrifice. No one ought to eat meat unless they are, at least in principle, prepared to kill it. But now, the small local abattoirs are going out of business; the visible connection between a live sheep and a cooked cheeseburger is becom-ing more and more tenuous. And it would seem that when herbivores are forced to be carnivores, by being given a diet of other herbivores' animal tissue, the resulting BSE crisis is a sign of nature's ability to revenge itself on too much manipulation of the distinctions built into the creation.

So there are some things that are given to us for our benefit. At the same time, there are many creatures that exist entirely in their own right, and obey the mandate to be fruitful and multiply without any involvement with us. But even in those distant centuries, our authors realized that we have responsibilities both to creatures with which we are directly involved, like sheep and cattle, and to the greater number of species with which we share the hospitality of the planet. And there are also those creatures which, with the best will in the world, we cannot avoid regarding as enemies. Will we, one day, see pickets standing outside our hospitals, carrying placards saying 'Justice for Viruses' or 'Liberation for Mosquitoes'? If length of residence is any basis for a claim, bacteria have more rights than any other living creatures. They have been around for millions of years longer than any of the rest of us. And, even if some of them get a bad press, we could not do without them. No bacteria at work, no other life. That is another angle on 'God at work'.

For Reflection

When you next get an opportunity to do so, go and look carefully at a mountain or hill. Who owns it? In what sense can anyone own it? Then look at the 'property' in which you live. Do you own it? Or are you a tenant? What is its value? If you are the owner, you may be able to find out the value of the land on which your home is built. Who has decided that value? Whether the owner is yourself or a landlord, what does 'ownership' mean? What are its limitations and responsibilities? And what about your local church? Ask the same questions about it.

Questions for Working Groups

1. What sorts of 'artists' are there in your group? In what ways are you working with God in being creative?

2. In what ways are you taking responsibility for the natural environment in your own area? Who is involved in, for instance, debates about genetic modification, the BSE crisis, hunting and blood-sports? How are you involved with your local authorities in their environmental responsibilities?

3. How far is your group involved with fair trade organizations?

4. The passage from Deuteronomy 26 (which is often read at Harvest) is, strictly, not about harvest (when 'all is safely gathered in') but about the firstfruits. It is about dedicating the first results of one's efforts at creating wealth. In the Anglican Calendar, this is traditionally celebrated on Lammas Day (1 August). Can you work out a way of making a meaningful celebration of Lammas, perhaps by making an offering of the first income we get from a new venture, or a token of the first wage in a new job?

4

Resting

Thus the heavens and the earth were finished, and all their multitude. And on the seventh day God finished the work that he had done, and he rested on the seventh day from all the work that he had done. So God blessed the seventh day and hallowed it, because on it God rested from all the work that he had done in creation.

These are the generations of the heavens and the earth when they were created.

Genesis 2:1–4a

On the face of it, the end of the sixth day is the climax of the story, for it sees the creation of human life. But the real climax is the seventh day. The seventh day takes us beyond anything which science can analyse. The climax of creation is not God's activity but God's rest. The climax of the Babylonian creation story told of the public glorification of the great god Marduk, as all the other gods proclaim his honour and his 50 names. The Hebrew story of Genesis takes the same framework, but tells simply of God's blessing and rest. This shows that our authors were interested not just in the fact that things have been made but in the evaluation of these things. Evaluation is recognizing value, celebrating value, taking time to notice it and rest in it and love it. This is, in a word, worship.

The account of the first six days follows a pattern familiar in science. It proceeds, as science does, by categorizing, by splitting up, by recognizing and labelling different parts of our environment. In the seventh day, it is all put together. We recognize that the most important things cannot be discovered from just looking at the bits and pieces. The total pattern is greater than the sum of the bits and pieces, and it is this which discloses the unifying purpose of God. It leads both to the worship of God and to the ordering of society in justice and a right sharing of the wealth of the earth. God's purpose is disclosed in the creation as a whole, not just in a few special places or 'coincidences', and not just at points where we can find no other explanation. God is God of the whole creation, or he is not God at all.

God values his creation, he reckons it to be good; this shows that we cannot divide his role of Creator from his role of maintainer. A God who merely sets the cosmic machine in motion and then sits back to watch it cannot be the God of the Bible, who continues to care for what he has made. The psalms that celebrate creation, such as Psalm 104, make this clear. God's creation is a continuous work as well as an originating initiative. We can accept that the universe is an unfinished process, in which hope is a proper element. God sees the creation as 'very good', but this is not to say that it is perfect, totally finished; it can mean that the creation is well set up for its purpose. It is all that God intends, as a total unity to proceed on its way. Its potential is as God wishes it to be. Our creed invites us to confess our faith in God as 'Maker of heaven and earth' – and 'maker' means both original maker and continuing maker. In some recent liturgies for baptism and confirmation, candidates are asked whether they believe in 'God the Father, who made the world', and then whether they believe in Jesus Christ, who redeemed mankind, and in the Holy Spirit, who gives life to the people of God. Then comes the announcement, 'This is the faith of the Church.' It is, I suppose, part of the faith of the Church, but it is a very weak statement. It implies that God's work in creation and Christ's work in redemption are both limited to the past; it implies that the work of Christ is limited to human beings and has no significance for the rest of Creation; and it implies that the Holy Spirit also has nothing to do with creation as a whole, and is interested only in Christians. If that is the faith of the Church, it is a pretty limited and dull thing to want to be baptized into. I have felt thoroughly embarrassed as the minister of this part of the Confirmation service.

The seventh day tells us that creation is about rest as well as about activity. But rest is not empty. Rest gives space for reflection and evaluation. Sabbath worship gives us an opportunity to look back and learn. When we come to worship on Sunday, we consciously bring with us in our spiritual briefcase at least four things: something to confess, something to give thanks for, something to pray about, and something to offer. Very good. This is sensible discipline for the individual worshipper. But does our corporate worship give us a chance to do this kind of reflection as a group? Does it give us space to reflect on our life as a community, not just for ourselves as a congregation but also as a parish – a parish in the proper sense of the word, a population within which the congregation is set? What has been going on in our area in the last few days? We pray about crises on the other side of the planet; what about our local Job Centre? We give thanks for the work of our medical staff; what about the transport system?

The seventh day tells us that rest is good in itself. It is not merely a time when we can recharge our batteries so that we can get on with the real job There are keen churchpeople who seem to be unable to take a break from ecclesiastical exercises, just as there are clergy who seem to be unable to retire and live without the role of authority which the clerical profession gives them. Such people no doubt earn some appreciation; but I am afraid that they may be in danger of obstructing the Sabbath vision, and the world is to that extent less joyful.

Sabbath worship is the worship of the one who was and is and will be Creator. It is not worship of nature itself. Those who seek to worship nature itself can easily overlook the shadow side of nature, its randomness and apparent cruelty. The worship of nature, or of the native spirit of the land, or any such element within the creation, is likely to make us tolerant of cruelty and to sanctify barriers and boundaries between us and other groups of people.

Sabbath worship is worship of the one Creator God. The Sabbath is equally for the employer, the employee and the unemployed; it is one day in seven when this sort of distinction is discontinued.[1] Keep the Sabbath, and avoid the risk of falling into slavery again. That is the message of the fourth commandment.

The seventh day explains why all the preceding activity is measured out in 'days'. The starting-point for our authors was the present experience of a week shaped around the seventh day. Days and months and years are natural units of time dictated to us by the lights of the sky, as indicated on the fourth 'day', but the week is a cultural invention. The seventh day is the supreme sign of God's authority and God's blessing. The point of saying that God created in six days is to give the highest possible authority to the fundamental difference represented by the seventh day, so as to insist on the authority of the seventh day as a mandate for the community that our authors were addressing. There would be no point in saying that God made the universe in 4000 years or 15 billion years and then rested; that would have no implication for our understanding of the shape of the week. It would not tell us that we need to make a weekly celebration of our deliverance from slavery.

For the Hebrews, the Sabbath stood for several other blessings. The Sabbath was every seventh year as well as every seventh day. In our Western systems, the academic high-fliers get 'sabbatical leave'; they are allowed time off work so as to fly a bit higher. In Hebrew law, the sabbatical year was time off work for ordinary citizens; every seven years they had a refresher course to enable them to catch up with a whole range of subjects included under the general heading of 'the law' – subjects such as medicine, hygiene, history, courtship and marriage, civil and criminal law, ritual, sanitation, agriculture, animal welfare, working conditions, the rights of aliens and asylum seekers, dietetics, census studies, theology, and so on. So, the gap between the scholar and the peasant is to be minimal, and there is to be no educational underclass. Knowledge is not to be restricted to those who can pay for it. Ordinary citizens are to be kept informed about their rights under the law; they can feel that the law can be on their side, and that therefore the Lawgiver can be on their side also.[2] God is the God of the second chance, the one who makes space for those who have missed out on previous opportunities.

The climax of the whole Sabbath system was the year of Jubilee, every 50 years. This was a festival of the rule of God, not the rule of any human monarch or aristocratic authority. It was an occasion for a regular straightening-out of the inequalities of society. Land could not be sold in perpetuity (or, as we would say today, freehold). All that could be sold was the use of it until the next Jubilee year. Then it returned to the custodianship of the family whose inheritance it was originally. So the community was to be protected from the emergence of a small landed oligarchy holding huge estates, on the one hand, with a large landless majority on the other hand. This also meant that debts had fixed terms; with due safeguards, there was to be a moment when existing debts would be cancelled and people could make a new start.[3] The motive for Sabbath and Jubilee springs directly from the community's experience of slavery. A great deal of enslavement has been directly due to indebtedness. The modern movement called Jubilee 2000, which campaigns for the cancellation of the unpayable debts of the poorest nations of the world, is correct to see a close connection between the movement to cancel debts and the movement to abolish slavery; it is also correct to claim a direct link between its campaign and the biblical principle of Jubilee. The law of Moses recognized a primary issue in economic ethics, namely that the problem is not how to get the rich to give to the poor but how to stop the rich from taking from the poor. The poor are not our problem; we are their problem.

God has given the earth to the human race – to the human race as a whole, not just to a privileged minority; this is a constant theme in the psalms. So when one group has too much and another has too little, that is simply theft. Consider the teaching of three of the most respected of the early theologians of the Church: 'The bread in your cupboard belongs to the hungry person; the coat hanging unused in your closet belongs to the person who needs it; the shoes rotting in your closet belong to the person who has no shoes; the money which you put in the bank belongs to the poor' (St Basil); 'Do not say, "I am using what belongs to me." You are using what belongs to others. All the wealth of the world belongs to you and to others in common, as the sun, air, earth, and all the rest' (St Chrysostom); 'It is not with your wealth that you give alms to the poor, but with a fraction of their own which you give back; for you are usurping for yourself something meant for the common good of all' (St Ambrose). And praise God that this is true; this is the kind of Creator that we believe in.[4]

The powerful will want to have a Sabbathless society,

because in such a society slaves are not released, production does not cease, the land has no rest, debts are never cancelled, exploitation is not curbed, an ignorant underclass is allowed to persist, the distinction between owners and non-owners is maintained, and nothing will interfere with the power of some people to act as managers of others.[5] The Sabbath is a joyful blessing, for all who are sensitive to the danger of enslavement. Above all, the Sabbath is a gift. It shows up the deepest division among human beings, the division between those who receive life as a gift and those who hold it as something to be grabbed.

In the experience of Jesus, the Sabbath had become a restriction, a weapon in the hands of people who did not wish to share in new creation. Jesus affirmed the original value and intention of the Sabbath. He healed on the Sabbath, and so healed the Sabbath itself. The great affirmation of the Christian gospel, in the activity of Jesus and in the preaching of Paul, remains a Sabbath message, namely that God is with those who can accept life as a gift and God has problems with those who want to have it as a restricted commodity. Graspers lose; those who are willing to accept gifts receive. Christians need to remember that all this is something which we owe to our older cousins, the Jews. We may think that our Easter Sunday supersedes the Sabbath. If we came to our Easter (or, for that matter, to our Christmas) with anything like the joy and light-heartedness with which some Jews celebrate the Sabbath, we would be notorious as the happiest people in the world.

The Sabbath is a day for the celebration of creation. Christians are not very good at this. One reason is that we are rightly keen to emphasize the new creation, and to celebrate Sunday, the day of resurrection. Another is that we remember, only too well, the way in which, both in the Gospels and in some Christian practice, 'Sabbath' has meant negation and restriction. Another is, perhaps, that

Christians are unwilling to be led by the spirituality of Judaism; there is a good deal more in the psalms than in most Christian hymnbooks about the celebration of creation. This fits in with John Polkinghorne's observation, 'Anyone constructing a service on a scientifically oriented theme will find much more choice of material in the psalter than in the hymnbook.'[6] A further possible reason is that to celebrate creation is something which appeals to laypeople, and therefore can be played down by the professional clergy. Creation involves every single person; the sacraments of redemption have become the specialism of the ordained, and they decide the liturgical programme. Harvest is a festival which continues to make an appeal to the general public, even if in a limited and prettified way; but some of the best-known harvest hymns are not really about harvest but about the Last Judgement! Our prayerbooks do contain a song called 'Benedicite'. It turns the orderly story of creation in the first chapter of Genesis into a joyful procession of praise. It calls on each of God's creatures – the nice ones and the nasty – to bless the Creator. One of the gloomier achievements of Christian worship has been to turn this Jewish celebratory parade into a dreary Lenten penance. There ought to be a prize for someone who can devise a way of making 'Benedicite' into a really effective liturgical experience. It could be a little contribution towards reviving the celebration of creation as part of Christian devotion.[7] The human voice is required to give expression to creation's praise; but we also recognize that, simply by existing, the other elements of creation have been engaged in the worship of the Creator for boundless aeons before human beings came on the scene. Humans come in late to share in the praise of God 'as it was in the beginning'.

Theologians speak of a 'doctrine' of creation. But the first article of our Creed is not just a prose statement; it is a celebration, it is something to sing. There is no theology without worship, there is no doctrine without wonder, there is no logic without surprise. Otherwise, however correct our words may be, they misrepresent the heart of things. A theology which does not raise the heart to sing, which does not inspire the will to struggle against enslavement and injustice, is not true to the foundation texts of theology. The Christian creed is a song of thanksgiving and commitment; dullness, rather than unorthodoxy, is the real betrayal of the Lord of creation. I have mentioned that Christian devotion has been rather poor in its expression of a celebration of creation, but there are exceptions. For example, there is St Francis's 'Canticle of Brother Sun', printed in many hymnbooks under the first line 'All creatures of our God and King'; notably, it includes the 'gentle sister, death' as a blessed part of creation. Then there is 'St Patrick's Breastplate', printed (although sometimes very incompletely) under the first line 'I bind unto myself today'. Finally, there is the anonymous early Welsh poem, 'Glorious God, I give you greeting'. This seems at first to be just a jumble of ideas; but it is a wonderful account of how all things, from their various starting-points, come together into a unity of praise. This is 'Benedicite', taken to a new level of inclusiveness.

Hail to you, Glorious Lord!
May church and chancel praise you,
May chancel and church praise you,
May plain and hill-side praise you,
May the three springs praise you,
May darkness and light praise you.
May the cedar and sweet fruit tree praise you.
Abraham praised you, founder of the faith.
May the life everlasting praise you,
May the birds and the bees praise you,
May the stubble and the grass praise you.

Aaron and Moses praised you:
May male and female praise you,
May the seven days and the stars praise you,
May the lower and upper air praise you,
May books and letters praise you,
May the fish in the river praise you,
May thought and action praise you,
May the sand and the earth praise you,
May all good things created praise you.
And I too shall praise you, Lord of glory:
Hail to you, Glorious Lord.[8]

For Reflection

A canal is a rather good image of the Sabbath rest. For it to
work properly, there has to be a gentle flow of water. If
there is no flow at all, the water will stagnate and disappear;
if the flow is too strong, vessels will have to use too much
power when moving in the opposite direction to the flow.
To get it right is a matter of skilful and sensitive design.
Unlike a road or railway, the water of the canal cannot go
uphill. When he built the Llangollen Canal 200 years ago,
with few sophisticated surveying instruments, Telford
engineered the whole 30-mile stretch from Llantysilio to
Whitchurch with only two locks. He had to construct two
massive aqueducts and three tunnels; but otherwise he built
the canal, even in the hilly Dee Valley, by clinging sensi-
tively to the varying contours of the landscape. The canal
belongs to the land; it is moulded and disciplined by it.

Questions for Working Groups

1. Do you really enjoy Sunday?

2. How far does your Sunday worship include the concerns of your area – its industries, its organization and administration, its various communities?

3. What do you feel about the remarks of St Ambrose, and the other theologians of the early Church, whom I have quoted, about ownership and sharing of wealth?

4. What signs do you see of the purpose of God as the giver of a second chance – in education, for instance, or in your church programme?

5. Look back to the last question for Chapter 1. Have you found any more good hymns or songs celebrating God as Creator?

5

Making a Model

In the day that the Lord God made the earth and the heavens, when no plant of the field was yet in the earth and no herb of the field had yet sprung up – for the Lord God had not caused it to rain on the earth, and there was no one to till the ground; but a stream would rise from the earth, and water the whole face of the ground – then the Lord God formed a man of dust from the ground, and breathed into his nostrils the breath of life; and the man became a living being.

Genesis 2:4a–7

Many years ago, I made a recording of a simple conversation. I have played it several times in study-groups, and then asked people to describe what they have heard. About half the members tell a sequential story – 'A said, B said, A said, B said', and so on. The others see the conversation more as two blocks of emotion in contact with each other – 'There was this fellow A and he was this kind of character and he had this kind of problem, and there was this lady B who was that kind of character and had that kind of problem'. Both versions are true. But they reflect two different kinds of hearing and two different kinds of storytelling. We find this kind of difference right here at the beginning of the Bible.

The account of Creation in Genesis chapter 1 is orderly, systematic and developmental, not tentative or experimental. It was a people who had been through the catastrophe of the exile who framed this great recital of the orderliness of the cosmos. It was a people who had been through the social fragmentation of mass removal who so majestically expressed the supreme authority of a reliable Creator. And their doctrine was not that once upon a time all had been well; rather, they were teaching: 'This is what is true about us now. In spite of all the appearances, all is well now; the one who creates us is also the one who saves us. This is a law-abiding universe.'

Now, at Genesis chapter 2, verse 5 onwards, we come to another account of creation. This is from an earlier period of Israel's history. Here, God is not so much the sovereign Lord of the universe as the experimenter, the deviser of new opportunities. God is testing out his creation, and is free to criticize it. He is concerned not so much about law as about relationships. His characteristic word is not 'Let there be light', but 'It is not good for the man to be alone'.

There is more than one way of expressing truth, especially when that truth is about the great matters of God's purpose and human identity. We shall notice detailed differences between the two versions as we proceed. The important thing for us to notice at this stage is that the later version has not replaced the older. The authors of the time of the Exile did not scrap the earlier version as being out of date or primitive, but they realized that there was scope for an alternative way of looking at the great theme of creation. At a still later stage, some editorial group came to the same conclusion, and decided to keep both versions in the canon of Scripture. So, right at the beginning of the Bible, we see the principle which scientists would call complementarity. If the subject under study is sufficiently large and varied, it is unlikely that one model or interpretative system will be sufficient to account for it. If we believe that there has been divine inspiration in the original writing of our biblical texts, we must recognize divine inspiration also at the editorial desks where decisions were made about what should be kept in the Scriptures and what should be kept out. The same principle applies concerning the witness about Jesus. The Gospel of John tells the story of Jesus in a very different way to the first three Gospels, but it does not displace them; it does not make them unnecessary or out of date. Different people will find themselves more at home in one version than another, and we will probably find that we move from one to the other at different stages of our lives.

God is generous to us in our variety. We rejoice in this. We should beware of using the word 'only' too much; 'only' is too often used as a way of saying that we are right and the others are wrong. 'Only' can be a way of reducing the truth. The science of acoustics can tell us how sounds are made and are transmitted to us, but if music is *only* a series of acoustic events, some of our knowledge is being stolen from us. Our thinking is a matter of chemical and electrical events in the brain; but if it is *only* that, there is no way of deciding whether our thinking is correct or incorrect – including our thinking about what happens when we think! We normally live on several levels of truth, and one version or interpretation is not sufficient. People who are truly bilingual have a major advantage at this point; they are used to moving easily from one set of terms to another, without confusion and without disrespect to either. They are linguistic amphibia. The Latin-English word 'translate' is a word of power; it implies that an idea has to be taken out of one language and transferred across into another. The corresponding Welsh word, 'cyfieithu', is gentler; it implies that the two languages rest together alongside each other. The editor of Genesis was content to be bilingual in this sense; as readers, we are encouraged to be spiritual amphibia.

At the same time, as well as this essential tolerance, there is a proper exclusiveness. There are other interpretations of creation, and of our relationship to God, which we have to say are not acceptable, as the scientist will exclude the idea which experiment shows to be unsound. Different as they are to each other, these two versions in Genesis both affirm that God is good, that the material world is real and important, that history has a purpose. Unless we hold onto these truths, we will lose our deepest reasons for giving fundamental value to persons. Scientific study would also lose some of its underlying resource. Archbishop William Temple claimed: 'It may be too much to argue, as some have done, that science is a fruit of Christianity, but it may be safely asserted that it can never spontaneously grow up in regions where the ruling principle of the Universe is believed to be either capricious or hostile.'[1]

The most obvious difference between the two accounts of creation is simply in their presentation of the sequence in which things are known. According to the first chapter, we humans come at the end, as the climax of a series; according to the second, we humans are the first living creatures to appear. There is little point in arguing about which came first, human beings or bacteria; that is not a live issue. But the real *Genesis* question, the *beginning* issue, is 'Where do we start?' Do we start with the Big Bang, and the things of evolutionary nature, and eventually arrive at ourselves? Or do we take the line that we ourselves are the most accessible clue to the nature of reality, and that this must be our point of departure? Both ways have their validity. Genesis 2 allows for the fact that I am myself the centre of perception of my world, and that without me there would be nothing for me to be conscious of. The essential question is not 'Is this an accurate account of the way things began?', but 'Does this correspond to the way that I experience myself and my environment?' The title 'Genesis', then, is not only

about the beginning of the universe; it is about the beginning question, the basic issue, the starting-point of our
enquiry. The study of human origins is inevitably a highly
specialized undertaking, and the non-specialist has to take
its findings on trust; but in the central questions about
humanity every person is a scientist and can contribute to
the continuing research, because the essential question is
about ourselves.

With our new author, the first thing that we notice is that
God has a new name. God has something like a personal
name – most accurately translated as 'Yahweh God'. We do
not start with a philosophical abstraction. We start, as the
Hebrews did, with an experience of one called Yahweh, for
whom the only fitting title was 'God'. Christians know the
nature of God in the person of the specific figure of Jesus of
Nazareth; in meeting Jesus, crucified and risen, they find
themselves exclaiming, with the Apostle Thomas, 'My Lord
and my God'.[2]

In the first chapter of Genesis, human beings are made in
the image of God. In this second chapter, God is much more
in the image of humans. He thinks and speaks like a person.
He is very much involved in the story. This story is more
like the stories which Jesus tells; the whole point of those
stories is that, as hearers, we have to take responsibility for
what we hear – as Jesus frequently insists.[3] In other words,
the hearer is trusted. Jesus seems not to have made many
theoretical statements about the Kingdom of God; he often
described the Kingdom by saying, 'It is *as if* ...', and then
told a story which illuminated just one aspect of the
Kingdom. This story will not tell us all that there is to know
about the creation. It can be picked up in ways which may
be misleading. We can find its truth; or we can obscure its
truth. Let us hear the authors describing the creation by
saying to us: 'It is *as if* ...' We are trusted with this story, to
make of it what we can.

In this story, when we first meet God, he is playing, like a person plays; indeed, who except a child would model a man out of the dust of a garden path? God is not only the powerful father; he is the playful child, and Christian faith tells us that it is through the *Son* that all things are made. At the heart of the creative activity of God, there is the character of the child, the character of intuition, of searching, exploring and learning. God is not only parent to us; he is also child to us. He is on the younger side of the parent–child divide, the tension which all of us carry around in some degree. About 20 years ago, when we started to become aware of the need to use inclusive language, some clergy took to replacing the word 'man' in the liturgy with the phrase 'men and women'; a conservative and witty friend of mine used to respond by calling out 'Unfair to children!' He was correctly insisting that the old meaning of the word 'man' (which he did not really want to discard) did include the *whole* human race; and he saw a danger that if you stress inclusiveness in one direction you may end up being exclusive in another. There is a real danger that our ways of thinking, of doing theology and of praying may allow no place for anyone who is not literate and over 21. In that case, we need to make space for the God-like, the child-like, in our devotion. We need, quite literally, more scope for modelling, for using clay and paint, for being artists, and for letting the child have the initiative. In our culture, the process is the other way round; through such things as computer games, adults are devising methods of making money by selling violence to children as a form of play. We are rightly aware of the more obviously vile and perverse ways in which adults abuse children; the corrupting of their play is also something which calls for a millstone to be tied around some necks and to be cast into the sea.

The first chapter of Genesis reminded us of the unimaginably large size of the universe. Now, we are told, God plays with the dust, with that which is unimaginably small. The nucleus of the atom is only a thousand-billionth of a centimetre in size. But this what we are made of – and the nucleus itself is made up of smaller components. The power of this 'dust' is expressed graphically by Theodosius Dobzhansky: 'The aggregate volume of all the genes in all the sex cells which produced the world's population today would probably not exceed that of a vitamin capsule. This tiny mass contains all the biological heredity of the living representatives of our species, and the material basis for its future evolution.'[4]

We are made out of the dust of the ground. The first chapter of Genesis tells us that we share in the creative process of the animal world. Now we are reminded of our direct links with the earth itself. The human being who is made is an 'adam'. He is described as a solitary male; the feminine of 'adam' is 'adamah', which is translated as 'ground'. That is the closeness of the relationship. The basic elements of which humans are made are not different to those of which the earth is made. Human and humus belong together. 'On Ilkley Moor baht'at' says it all.

Dust is gathered, and dust is scattered. We are made out of impermanent, insecure material. Our hope is not that some kind of permanence can be given to this obsolescent material. We return to dust; our hope is not for immortality but for resurrection, not for preservation but for transformation, not for an infinite prolonging of the old creation but for a new creation. The same God who created the old will be creating the new.

At the beginning of the story, there is no vegetation, no rain and no one to work. But there is some hidden source of water, and so there is a possibility for the earth. In the first chapter, water is the dangerous, threatening stuff which has to be given boundaries. Hebrew people were not fond of the sea; it represented danger, insecurity, foreignness.[5] So, for the authors of the first chapter, the Creator saves us from the ocean; everything was terribly wet water before God acted. In the second chapter, water is a blessing; the Creator saves us from the desert; everything was terribly dry earth before God acted. This would surely appeal to the people of the area referred to in this story, the area of Mesopotamia. In addition to all their other problems in the last few years, the people of Baghdad have been faced with the steady lowering of the water-level of the Tigris. Water is the most wonderful symbol of the potential of creation. You yourself are nearly 80% water. It is like that attractive definition of hydrogen: a light colourless gas which, given sufficient time – say, 15 billion years – can become the Chancellor of the Exchequer.

In the desert, God makes his earthy doll, and breathes spirit into it; the adam becomes a living being. The Hebrew language does not enable a distinction between 'body' and 'soul'. The translation, 'the man became a living being' is right. Even if we use the word 'soul', as in the Authorised Version, the statement is 'man *became* a living soul', not 'man was given a soul'. The distinction is not between 'body' and 'soul', as if 'soul' were a distinct property of the person; the distinction is between livingness and non-livingness.

This human being is the first living being; all life is due to the breath, or spirit, of God. That is the message of the story. A body without a spirit is a corpse and a spirit without a body is a ghost; neither is alive and neither can do anything useful. Therefore, if Christ is alive, he must have a body, in some way. That is why we say that his continued presence among us is in a body, in the Church, the Body of Christ.

✳

And the Lord God planted a garden in Eden, in the east;
and there he put the man whom he had formed. Out of
the ground the Lord God made to grow every tree that is
pleasant to the sight and good for food, the tree of life
also in the midst of the garden, and the tree of the knowl-
edge of good and evil.

Genesis 2:8–9

Immediately after the creation of the human being, we are
told of the creation of vegetable life. In the first chapter, the
created things have their own validity; trees and plants exist
for their own sake; they are in business to propagate their
own species; there is at first no observer or user of them.
In this second chapter, nothing exists until there is an
observer; when the observer arrives, other things come into
existence in roughly the same order as in the first chapter;
but they are seen from the observer's point of view. The
trees are valued first for their beauty, and then for their
provision of food.

We value things according to their value for us, rather
than for their intrinsic value. This is the assumption of this
second chapter. When we do this, we attach a value-added
worth to the thing concerned. We may almost give a
magical value to it. We give it meaning. 'That tree is a
conifer'; 'That tree is a young larch'; 'That tree would be
worth £80 at the sawmill'; 'Turn right at that tree if you
want to find the public toilets'; 'Under that tree is where we
first made love'; 'That is the tree of the knowledge of good
and evil'. Meanings and labels of this kind fit easily into
the world-view of this chapter; they would not do so in the
world-view of the writers of the first chapter.

After the making of the human being, God's next task is
to make a garden, or park. Our authors see the making of a

garden as a specially divine activity. It follows a process which the Creator has first followed. Nelson Mandela tells of the new lease of life which he gained on Robben Island when he was allowed to make a garden.

> A garden was one of the few things in prison that one could control ... The sense of being the custodian of this small patch of earth offered a small taste of freedom. In some ways, I saw the garden as a metaphor for certain aspects of my life. A leader must also tend his garden; he, too, sows seeds, and then watches, cultivates, and harvests the result. Like the gardener, a leader must take responsibility for what he cultivates; he must mind his work, try to repel enemies, preserve what can be preserved and eliminate what cannot succeed.[6]

This is a practical, unsentimental estimate of the meaning of a garden; it fits well with the botanical parables of the one who, in his risen presence, was identified by Mary Magdelene as the gardener.

The idea of the Garden of Eden would make the grandest appeal to people set in the sort of conditions suggested in this story. Out of the arid landscape, a cultivated and fertile park is formed. The man can be happily occupied there; life is not going to be idleness, but neither is it going to be one long grind.

Eden is away to the east. The east was not a place to which the Hebrews looked with much affection, since too many enemies and rivals lived there. But they knew that their ancestor Abraham came from the east; perhaps they had a general historic sense that civilization and language came to them from the east. Certainly we Westerners need to remember that it is to the East that we owe the origin of almost all the riches of our culture, our science and our faith.

'Eden' in Hebrew implies delight or pleasure. When the text was put into Greek, translators took a Persian word meaning an enclosure, and from this we get our word 'Paradise'. Jews of the time of Jesus knew this word, and thought of it as the forecourt of the place of final resurrection, the location for the renewing act of God. So Jesus announces it as his meeting-place with the penitent thief. Christ, the Second Adam, makes this appointment, not for a day in the far distant future, but for 'today'. He makes the appointment with a convicted terrorist. The one person on the Golgotha scene who can recognize the true kingly authority of Jesus is this one who has spent his life in opposition to kings and authorities and all that they stand for. He finds himself strung up alongside one who is explicitly labelled as 'King of the Jews'. At first he merely curses. But then he recognizes that this king is sharing his execution; he is also being given the treatment imposed by counter-revolutionary authority on people who are threats to public order. Here at last is a king who makes sense. He asks to be remembered by this king. And he hears the promise; he is the first to enter Paradise. In our Paradise, our garden of Eden, he is the first citizen.[7]

Paradise is the forecourt of the resurrection. This is where the crucified Lord met the 'spirits in prison', in the account of the day after Good Friday given in 1 Peter 3. Christ, we say, 'descended into Hell'. He claimed his place among his ancestors, and among the ancestors of us all, as lord and comrade of them all. Most enmities among the human race depend on our ancestry. We feel hostile to the other group because of what they did, long ago, to our group – Catholics or Protestants, Arabs or Crusaders, slaves or slave-owners, Christians and non-Christians. We owe it to our ancestors to honour their sacrifice and to keep the memory alive in our generation. Some of us need to be reconciled to our own ancestors; others need to be reconciled to new and strange neighbours, whose ancestors were enemies of our ancestors. Christ is no stranger to either group. He meets them as deliverer and friend. In Christ we can all find the truth, which was so intensely expressed by Wilfred Owen when he described the meeting between two soldiers of opposing armies, killed in the same battle: 'I am the enemy you killed, my friend.'[8] Paradise remains as a symbol of the eternal purpose of God, which is not thwarted by our enmities and disbeliefs. So the churches of Southern and Central Africa include in their liturgy this prayer to Christ: 'You open and none can shut; open the gates of your kingdom to those who have died without hearing your gospel.'

Our story recognizes four basic human needs, and they come in the following order: territory, activity, food, and companionship. First, the man is given a place to live in. Only when this territorial instinct is satisfied do we move on to the other needs. One of the subtlest forms of cruelty is to keep people insecure in respect of territory and home. There are some people who can tolerate and even choose this sort of insecurity, just as there are some who can positively choose celibacy. But it is difficult to imagine anything more calculated to cut at the roots of a person's security than to insist on a system which shunts people around and condemns them to involuntary homelessness.

A river flows out of Eden to water the garden, and from there it divides and becomes four branches. The name of the first is Pishon; it is the one that flows around the whole land of Havilah, where there is gold; and the gold of that land is good; bdellium and onyx stone are there. The name of the second river is Gihon; it is the one that flows around the whole land of Cush. The name of the

*third river is Tigris, which flows east of Assyria. And the
fourth river is the Euphrates.*

Genesis 2:10–14

A territory without irrigation would be no blessing. Water
flows out of Eden for the benefit of the garden; it then flows
on and divides into four rivers. In effect, the whole earth is
nourished by water from a single source. Wise people make
sure that they are informed about the source of their water-
supply, and also about where the drains lie. An abundance
of water is the greatest natural blessing. The river of
Paradise was so abundant that the overflow from it could
nourish the whole known world. All the goodness that we
humans can perceive is merely the overflow of the goodness
in the heart of God.

Until recently, it would be unheard of for a human
settlement of any size to be built in a place where there is no
river or sea. The first such city to be built was Johannes-
burg, about 115 years ago. And why? 'Because the gold of
that land is good.' Water and minerals are most basic
reasons why people choose certain places to create settle-
ments.

*

*The Lord God took the man and put him in the garden of
Eden to till it and keep it. And the Lord God commanded the man,*
   *'You may freely eat of every tree of the garden; but of
   the tree of the knowledge of good and evil you shall
   not eat, for in the day that you eat of it you shall die.'*

Genesis 2:15–17

God's human creation needs to work. Adam is put into the garden with a job. We are not designed to live on bread alone; we are designed to work. 'Productivity' is the aim; but what is gained if one company increases its productivity by causing more members of society to be unproductive? When people are given the terrible label 'redundant', it is a disorder not only for the unemployed individual but for the whole of society. We are all hurt when some of our members have to live with this very painful form of unwantedness. The words here in Genesis 2 are different to the words of the first chapter, but the message is the same. We are designed to be stewards of the rest of creation, to serve it, to take responsibility for it, to work. The same authority who gives living-space also gives the opportunity for work. Adam lives above the shop; his right to live and his right to work belong together. He is not a mere labour-unit which can be discarded when his period of profitable usefulness is over. His work is necessary for the maintenance of the creation. It is good. It is worth doing. We are certainly right to give attention to questions of health and safety, to issues of proper pay, of differentials, of pension rights, of holiday entitlement and sickness benefit, and all the safeguards of modern employment practice. This continues to be necessary because of the constant possibilities of exploitation, intentional and unintentional. But how often do we see any exploration of the question of whether the work is actually worth doing, in itself?

God's human creation needs to eat. So there are fruit-trees, trees which satisfy the human desire for beauty and the human need for nourishment. But this story is fundamentally about meaning; some trees have significance which goes far beyond their physical function. They are at the centre, representing God as the source of life and of moral judgement. These are to be observed, not seized as the man's rightful property. He has to realize that they are at the centre of the garden, and that he is not. He is steward; everything is on loan to him. He is in the garden by invitation. God is the host.

So there is a prohibition in respect of one tree. There is a limit on Adam's range of activity. For the most part, he is entirely free. God's primary word to him is permission to live, to work, to eat. The command 'you shall not ...' is not the centre of God's will. The centre of God's will for marriage, for instance, is not the prohibition of adultery. If the marriage is healthy, the prohibition of adultery is virtually irrelevant; what matters is the divine permission, the divine grace, the divine freedom given to two people to explore the vast realm that is opened up by marriage. But there is a tree with a prohibition nailed to it, and a label. It is the tree of the knowledge of good and evil. What can this mean to someone in Adam's situation? He has no experience with which to interpret the words. Everything around is good. Every tree is a tree of goodness. Evil has no presence. But in the tree of the knowledge of good and evil there is another kind of goodness, the kind of goodness which needs badness to differentiate it and identify it. Goodness and evil are not equally basic or permanent. There is goodness before there is badness; badness is parasitic on goodness; forged currency depends on the existence of a system of good currency, but good currency is possible without the existence of forged currency. We can distinguish between goodness which is known only in contradistinction to evil and goodness which is simply goodness; there is not the same distinction in the case of evil, which does not have the same autonomy as goodness. That is why we can claim that there is a 'problem' of evil but not a corresponding problem of good. This is represented in Christian symbolism by the relationship between God and the Devil. The Devil is not the equal and opposite of God. The Devil is not a figure of eternity. The opposite number to the Devil is not God but

Michael the Archangel, the leader of the hosts of heaven. Satan and Michael are on the same level of creation, but one is corrupted and the other is consecrated. Evil is a product of something good, something which is claiming rights which are higher than what is true for it. It is goodness corrupted and thwarted. It can spoil everything within its range, but it depends on a supply of good things to corrupt and ruin; it cannot create them. There was, doubtless, competence in physics and economics in the design and administration of Auschwitz. Science may try to be independent of moral questions; it may prefer not to be aware of the tree of the knowledge of good and evil. But since Hiroshima, some scientists themselves acknowledge that science has lost its innocence.

'Knowledge', for the Hebrew people, was not a matter of information or abstraction. Knowledge is an action; most specially, it is the action of woman and man 'knowing' each other in sexual intercourse. Knowledge is experience, competence, practical justice. Knowledge of good and evil is not to be got from a book. The connection between eating and knowing is not arbitrary or magical; the action of infringing the prohibition is itself the knowing. The 'knowing' is not a form of maturity; 'knowing' good and evil in this sense is an inhibition, it is a restriction, a bind. It is the constant demand for endless assessment of motive, the hourly reappraisal of one's purity, the over-scrupulous lack of confidence in one's own judgement, the experiencing of 'good and evil' as an obstruction on one's ability to make a decision and get on with the work in hand – these are the signs of the inhibiting kind of knowledge which gets in the way of lively obedience and of cheerful holiness. It is a kind of death. To be dead, as St Paul saw, is to see life and opportunities and goodness not as grace but as burden, not as gift but as reward. To be dead means to live under compulsion, to have life as a problem. This kind of deadness cannot be healed by bold acts of will or scrupulous obedience to rules. We see the response in the person of Christ; far from seeking to escape from the binds and inhibitions of our condition, he immersed himself all the more deeply in them. He suffered from people whose zeal for goodness drove them to distrust and eventually destroy him. If you put on one side the assumption that everything which Jesus did was 100% obviously perfect, you will find that there are plenty of ambiguities in his behaviour. What about the money-changers in the Temple? They were only getting on with their usual routine. What about Pilate? Pilate gets the blame for a judicial murder which Jesus could perfectly well have avoided if he had chosen to do so. We say that Jesus was without sin; so he did the right thing in that he did not allow himself to get sidetracked away from the priorities of the Kingdom of God. But, in a world of moral ambiguities, the right thing often seems not to be the ideal thing. Jesus saw more sharply than anyone the absolute of goodness; it was a real part of his lifelong cross-bearing that he was not able always to do the absolutely ideal thing, that he was involved in a world of moral contradictions just as we are. But he met the evil head on, and was not trapped into inaction by the inhibiting rope of the knowledge of good and evil.

For Reflection

In 1993, to celebrate the centenary of the birth of the Shropshire poet Wilfred Owen, and also to mark the seventy-fifth anniversary of his death in action in France a week before the end of the 1914–18 war, the Wilfred Owen Association organized a competition for a memorial sculpture to the poet, to be built in the grounds of Shrewsbury Abbey. We offered a dozen or more extracts from the poems for the sculptors to choose from, to be used for the inscription. Without exception, they all selected the line from the poem 'Strange Meeting': 'I am the enemy you killed, my friend.' Paul de Monchaux's winning design has been built at Shrewsbury Abbey; it is based on the theme of a bridge, which recalls the pontoon bridge which Owen was trying to establish in enemy territory when he was killed. It represents a bridge between enemies, a bridge between languages and faith-systems, and a bridge between the living and the dead. There is full information about the significance of the memorial, together with the text of the poem, on a board nearby. The memorial would be a good place for reflection on the meaning of Paradise.

I can add a further dimension, which is not on any information board. In the summer of 2000, I arranged for a very international Israeli choir from Tel Aviv to sing a Hebrew prayer standing around this memorial. The conductor of the choir, Eli Gefen, had come to Israel as a refugee from Nazi-controlled central Europe, just before the Second World War. Eli served with the British army during the war. When he returned to Israel, he discovered that his closest boyhood friend, Zvi Ben-Yaakov, had been killed in action as a parachutist, when he was trying to get into Hungary to organize the rescue of other Jews. Eli was at that time working as a builder, and he was asked to build a memorial to Zvi Ben-Yaakov in a kibbutz near Haifa. For the inscription on that memorial, he took words from an Israeli poet, Chana Senesh; she also had been a trained parachutist, and had been shot on the same mission as Zvi. For the song at the Wilfred Owen memorial, Eli again chose words from Chana Senesh. This seemed to be exactly appropriate, and perfectly planned. What none of us could have known in advance was that our memorial to Wilfred Owen should turn out to be the mirror-image of the memorial built by Eli Gefen to his friend Zvi Ben-Yaakov 50 years earlier, in a kibbutz near Haifa, inscribed with words from Chana Senesh. To me, this story underlines the sense that the Wilfred Owen memorial at Shrewsbury is a rich symbol of the meaning of Paradise.

Questions for Working Groups

1. When I was a bishop, a group of laypeople used to meet regularly at our house to share their understanding of the meaning of their faith in relation to their work. It made me think that human work can be, very roughly, divided between work which is done because the creation is happening successfully (farmers, teachers, sheetmetal workers, drivers, midwives, registrars, etc.) and work which is required because the creation is going wrong (prison officers, probation officers, police, tax inspectors, customs and excise, barristers, etc.). (There are, of course, many who really fit in both these categories, such as doctors, politicians, development workers, etc.) Whatever you think of this, as a group of people with a wide experience of different kinds of work, what do you think human work is for? How do you judge whether a job is worth doing?

2. Rogation Sunday comes, conveniently, just before Ascension Day, when we celebrate Christ as Lord of earth and heaven. It is a good opportunity for recognizing and affirming all the various kinds of work which are done by people within the parish. Can you

develop the Rogation Day celebration along these lines? Can you, for instance, have a 'Stations of the Parish' in your church – a series of displays of the various enterprises happening in the area, with appropriate prayers? You could make a semi-permanent display, suggesting prayers for a wide range of people, with their names and, if possible, their photographs. The list would include: your bishop, parish priest, readers, wardens; ministers of other churches; your MP and MEP; your representatives in such bodies as the Scottish Parliament or Welsh Assembly; your representatives in County and District and Borough and Parish and Community Councils; your local school teachers and medical practitioners; and representatives of other institutions and organisations in the areas. Visitors to your church will see from this that you do have a real ministry to the community as a whole; they should be inspired to join you in your commitment of prayer.

6

Experimenting

Then the Lord God said,
 'It is not good that the man should be alone: I will give
 him a helper as his partner.'
So out of the ground God formed every animal of the
field and every bird of the air, and brought them to
the man to see what he would call them; and whatever
the man called every living creature, that was its name.
The man gave names to all cattle, and to the birds of the
air, and to every animal of the field; but for the man there
was not found a helper as his partner.

Genesis 2:18–20

So far in this second chapter of Genesis, we have heard of a permission and a prohibition from the mouth of God. Now we have a statement. God's first statement is indeed a statement of great significance: 'It is not good for the man to be alone.'

God is the critic of his own work. Like a painter, he stands back from his work. And he sees something which he cannot call 'very good'.

God is not only the one who starts things; he makes a response to things. He does not merely keep things in place; he causes change.

God sees what is wrong. To be alone is to be helpless. God decides to provide a partner and a helper.

The first man Adam was alone, and this aloneness is something from which God seeks to rescue us. The community of God's people is called to recognize the isolation between person and person as a sign that creation is incomplete. Christ comes to heal our isolation, to make the bridge across our various kinds of separateness. The whole mission of the Church is to express this purpose. God does not want us to be alone.

But Christ, the Second Adam, was alone; those who are called to follow Christ also find themselves to be alone. Jesus was able to be alone. The threat of isolation was not so terrible to him that it dominated his life. He did not depend upon a fan-club. He was able to lose friends and to fail to influence people.

Many people seek fellowship because they are afraid to be alone ... Let him who cannot be alone beware of community. He will only do harm to himself and to the community ... But the reverse is also true. Let him who is not in community beware of being alone ... Only as we are within the fellowship can we be alone, and only he that is alone can live in the fellowship.[1]

One of the most splendid stories in the New Testament, especially for Africans, is the story of the Chancellor of the Exchequer of Ethiopia: as a man used to an environment of power and prestige, he was intrigued by a message in Scripture which indicated that the divine was to be found in an isolated character who was treated as rubbish by the powerful. Philip's exposition made such sense that the Ethiopian asked for baptism. Having been baptized, he did not turn round and join the little company of believers in Jerusalem, but happily went on southward into a territory which some have called the Dark Continent, alone. Millions of Africans see him as 'our' ancestor in faith.[2]

It may well be good for us to be alone, if we are sharing the aloneness of Christ. There are certainly Christians who are called to be alone – as, for instance, a man I knew many years ago who was sure that his calling as a Christian was to be in his Union meeting on a Sunday morning, at the same time as the parish communion.

But here, in the original human condition, it is not good for the man to be alone. God does not have the instant solution up his sleeve. God has set himself a problem, and he does not know the answer.

God conducts some experiments with animals. A good attempt, but not good enough. Animals are indeed possible companions; they are of the same origin as the man, out of the earth. But they have not received the breath (or Spirit) of God. There cannot be true reciprocity between the man and the animals. The relationship is on the man's terms. The animals are not adequate as partners.

God makes all sorts of living creatures, and brings them to the man for comment and naming. The man has the ability to make words, to put differentiation onto the flow of things which appear before him. He isolates and identifies a thing, in distinction from other things. He creates language. The language is created in response to experience; the man sees the creature before he gives it a name. We who inherit language accept it on the authority of our parents and teachers. We often learn the word before we see the thing. This is fine, if language is simply to be an instrument for affirming the authority of the old. Also it is good, inasmuch as it tells us what to look for. But children are natural language-makers, and this creativity is easily stifled if the adults know everything in advance. It is probably a good thing that there are so many words, especially in computing, which children know and I don't know. New inventions require new names, so we have to come to terms with words such as megapixel and firewire. Similarly, we could say that God is bringing all sorts of subatomic things to human beings, and they are calling them names such as 'quark' and 'lepton', even before they are totally sure of their existence.

God, therefore, is giving permission to the human creature to make language, which is more than can be said for human beings themselves. In1536, Henry VIII's Act of Union of England and Wales deprived the Welsh language of legal status. Within living memory, Welsh-speaking children were penalized at school, with the same educational tricks with which the English-speaking administration in South Africa tried to kill Afrikaans a century ago. In our own day, there are schools which obstruct deaf children in the use of their 'native language' – the language of visual signs which is their natural manner of communication.

Language is a precious human gift, and God trusts us to use it as we meet his creation. But, like so many other things, it can be used as a means of control and domination, as a way of forcing people into a mould which suits the interests of those who have power. We assume that there are population-units called 'nations', and that these are defined by boundaries. Who decides what is a boundary? The boundary between South Africa and Lesotho is the Caledon River. One side of the river is labelled 'Lesotho', the other is labelled 'South Africa'. But traditionally both sides were occupied by the Basotho people; the labelling means that the Basotho have lost most of their traditional grazing land, and as a community are economically subservient to South Africa. But the boundary is there, in the language of politics and of maps. It has been a useful instrument in the hands of the conquerors. Nearer home, our geographical language may not be so obviously an instrument of oppression. But it still may be worth asking, for instance, what does it mean that Bronington is in Wales and Oswestry is in England?

Nature itself is a continuum; human language imposes a pattern or scheme of reference where there is not necessarily any objective basis for it. The colour spectrum is a continuum of wavelengths; what do we do with it? English divides it into seven, Zulu into four. English has perhaps a half-dozen words to describe the markings of animals; Zulu has over 300. The philosopher John Locke maintained that the boundaries between the various species of animals were so vague that they really had no separate existence at all; they were the creation of the human mind as it tried to impose order onto nature.[3] This naming and categorizing is the basis of any scientific activity – the development of an agreed set of terms. Words are tools, not masters. Theologians need to bear this in mind as much as anyone.

We need also to recognize that our competence in language is limited. We see and feel a lot more than we can communicate. The most important things sometimes find us most inarticulate. A great deal of our brain-power goes into our ability to recognize faces and voices; this clearly must have been useful to us in the evolution of our species. But most of us find it difficult to describe a person's face, because most of us have not developed precise terms with which to do so. Ask the police, who have to make identikits from people's descriptions! I am often surprised by people's skill in recognizing a voice on the telephone; but can you tell me *how* to recognize your voice? And how accurately do you think you can describe an indigestion pain?

The story tells us of the work of the man in giving names and making symbols. He has been brought in as an associate of God, in forming a pattern of meaning out of the flow of experience that has been coming at him. He is not impartial or disinterested; he is not compiling a dictionary. He is looking for a partner, and his work of naming is shaped by his hopes and his failures in this search. He is not concerned about the origins and structures of the creatures, but with their potential relationship to himself. He does not create them; he receives them from the Creator. But he does take responsibility for making an orderly classification of them. He creates categories, and this is the beginning of the making of scientific 'laws'. With this skill, he will be able to develop knowledge about what things are, how they have become, and how they can be used. But this will not, in itself, tell him how the knowledge is to be employed.

The authors and first readers of this chapter knew very well what cattle were good for. They knew about the usefulness and lack of usefulness of the birds and wild animals. They would understand, therefore, what Adam was really looking for; and this was something that these creatures could not supply. If, for instance, he was really looking for extra muscle-power to enable him to till the ground, he would be entirely satisfied with cattle. What he is looking for is something more than a functionary. Adam is human, with human needs. Like God, he is a being who can ask about what is not.

The arrival of the human is the arrival of thought. It is the arrival of experimentation and of doubt. In the human being, the world has a being who can judge and criticize it. To doubt means to put questions against one's experience and one's past. Adam's experience at this stage is an experience of discouragement and failure. The most reasonable deduction from this experience would be that his search is never going to be successful, and that no partner is ever going to be found. It is his doubt in the validity of this deduction that keeps him going. Where there is doubt there is hope. For people who have grown up in places of political or cultural security, doubt may seem to be a threat and an enemy. For people whose daily experience is of suffering, rejection, slavery, or death, any worthwhile faith will be a great stimulus to doubt, a demand to question the inevitability of their bondage.

Even the most privileged and secure of us will die. Death is the most certain fact of life, for prince and pauper alike. True faith calls us to doubt that death is indeed the most important thing about us. To believe in resurrection is to doubt the supremacy of the most obviously true fact about us. For most of us, who are set in a world of death and disorder, the community of faith is needed as a training-ground in responsible doubting. For the privileged, such as those who have the freedom to be interested in writing and reading theological books, doubt may seem to be a threat to faith. But, for the majority of humankind, doubt is an essential armour against despair.

Adam comes as a responsible critic into his environment. He is able to tolerate dissatisfaction. He is able to live in uncertainty. He does not settle for saying 'Yes' when he should say 'No'. He is a person of faith. Faith is not a thing to have, it is a willingness not to have. It is trust in what may be. It is not having but seeking.[4]

So the Lord God caused a deep sleep to fall upon the man, and he slept; then he took one of his ribs and closed up its place with flesh. And the rib that the Lord God had taken from the man he made into a woman and brought her to the man. Then the man said,
  'This at last is bone of my bones
  And flesh of my flesh;
  This one shall be called woman
  For out of Man this one was taken.'

Genesis 2:21–23

God is in charge of the experiment. He realizes that there is no solution for the problem in just trying out more and more of the available creatures. None of them is going to be a partner; none of them is going to be able to be in a reciprocal relationship with Adam. So God makes a new creation. He does not make another Adam; he does not go back to the manufacture of clay dolls. He tries a new method. He splits off part of Adam, and makes a new human being. Creation comes from division. Creation comes through the manipulation, modification and development of what is already there.

Adam cannot observe the process; he is heavily anaesthetized. He is in a state of not-knowing; he is in darkness. It is at this level, a level deeper than the conscious, that God's creative activity takes place. God's activity is not observed; it is known by its effect. The resurrection of the Second Adam was watched by no one. There were no video cameras or tape-recorders in the garden of Easter. We know of the new creation also by means of its effects.

This story is the man's story, Adam's story. Men have been in charge of the media. Most of the Bible has been written by men. They have organized and controlled the means of publication, and we may feel that it is biased and incomplete. In many cultures, women have preserved alternative traditions, which have been passed on orally among themselves, while they have gathered at wells and ovens; and these have been the stories which children have heard. Who can tell whether there were other accounts of the creation of male and female persons by the God of Israel, which have not survived? Steve Biko was, of all the generation of South African students of the 1960s, the one who was the most promising for the future, in terms of his courage, integrity and vision; his murder by the police on September 12 1977 was the most catastrophic waste. In his view, the worst thing that the whites had done to his people – worse than low wages and the lack of education and franchise, worse even than the theft of land – was the suppression of the African people's stories. Have women's stories been similarly suppressed?

The story in Genesis chapter 2 is told from the man's point of view (We shall note that this in fact leads to a surprising corrective to male-supremacy assumptions at one important point.) This is one reason for being thankful that there is a different stress, as we have already noticed, in the first chapter, where the female and the male in human creation are equally and together created in the image of God. But here, in the older story in chapter 2, Adam, the male, is created first, and it is because of his need that the female is created. Now, I cannot represent all points of view. I also am a male, and during my adult life I have been responding in delight and puzzlement and, sometimes, fear, to that extraordinary and wonderful creation: the human female. So, in my incompleteness, I do not apologize for the fact that I find that this old story speaks to me in the depths. It is not just that the other sex is attractive; we are made for each other and are involved in each other; we seek for a unity in each other which is not just to recapture something from the far-off origins but is the truth about ourselves as we are now, in our created nature under God.

Adam, in his investigations with the animals, has been looking for something which will satisfy his own conscious needs. He has had a job specification in mind, as he has been examining the candidates. With the appearance of Woman, this is all forgotten. Some people like to think that he acted as a perfect gentleman and politely introduced himself (in English, of course) with the neat palindrome, 'Madam, I'm Adam'. Indeed the traditional translations do rather suggest that Adam responded to the lady's appearance in grave and measured tones. The original Hebrew is much less inhibited. It is an exclamation, an explosion:

WOW!!! This is it! At last! Something has hit him that goes way beyond any assessment, any calculation, any introspection; something that breaks the boundaries of grammar. According to this story, this cry of ecstasy is the first human utterance. It is in verse-form; it is the first poem in human history. It is the basis of every love-song ever sung.

As we read this story, we may well feel that there are points where it is at odds with reality. We are grateful, as I have said, for the fact that there is an alternative account of creation which tells of the creation of male and female together. Even St Paul gets a bit mixed up in his handling of this second chapter: at first, he accepts its implication that the male is made first; but then he corrects it, from real experience of how life works. Then, from a text which at first tells of the subordination of woman, he insists on the true equality and interdependence of woman and man.[5]

A story of this kind cannot represent the whole truth. Let us claim from this story the primary points which it is emphasizing: first, the sense of loneliness and incompleteness of the human being in solitariness; second, the sense of wonder and delight when members of the opposite sex truly meet each other, the sense of the conclusion of a search, the sense that we find not just a functionary but one who is as entirely human as ourselves.

The story is expressed from Adam's point of view. The storyteller is, presumably, male, and sees himself as Adam, the first person on earth. As a reader, I am the first person. I accept the story as being about me, because I am the first person in my universe. Before me, the I which I call 'me' did not exist. Every other person that I meet is someone brought to me by the Creator. Every woman that I meet is in a very particular way someone brought to me by the

Creator. So I ask myself, is this story true about me, or isn't it?

The man has been looking for a helper, a functionary. He has been shopping around among the other creatures and found no satisfaction. With hindsight, we can see that he has been looking for the wrong thing. It would be no use giving him a lesson about this; it is not something that can be taught from a book. Nevertheless, he is not so bound up with his expectation that he fails to recognize the true answer when it appears. As soon as he meets the other person, he forgets his search for a functionary. He does not say, 'Ah, at last, a suitable assistant, bedmate, housekeeper, nurse.' He says, 'At last, here is someone who is really part of me; with her I am not going to be able to tell the difference between loving and being loved.' This is the reason behind the words of commitment in the marriage service. We do not say, 'I give myself to you (and you had better be as generous to me in return)', but 'I take you ...'; I accept you as I know you to be and as part of myself. I accept you until death us do part. I accept this person not just for as long as she fulfils certain functions, but until she ceases to be. We are bone of each other's bone. I need not be afraid of that which is so bound up with my own tissue. I can risk being fundamentally involved with this other person. A fear of this sort of involvement keeps all sorts of people in business; it provides a market for methods of identifying woman as only a functionary or a plaything. It seems to be a particular problem for males; it is the male Adam who makes this breakthrough, with his recognition 'bone of my bone, flesh of my flesh'.

'Bone of my bone' means that I have what she has and she has what I have. Jealousy is my fear that what she has cannot be mine; in return, it is my belief that she will be unable to accept what is mine. If she is bone of my bone, what I have and what she has will become ours together, and cannot be used to divide us from each other.

'Bone of my bone' is a discovery about myself. 'A person is a person through other persons.' This proverb of black South Africans sums up what is meant by the deep mysterious quality called *ubuntu*, the fundamental quality of being human. The other person is the presence of myself in that other person. In the other person, I can recognize things of myself which were previously hidden from me. I am known from the inside, from areas deeper than skin and tissue. My involvement with her means that I can live with fewer illusions about myself. The area of myself which I do know becomes reconciled to the areas of myself which I do not know and dare not know. This is true disillusionment; the fact that 'disillusionment' is so often seen as a sign of something wrong is the measure of our need for healing. Love rejoices in the truth.[6] God is love; so God is the entirely disillusioned one.

Adam gives the woman a name, as he did with the animals. But there is a great difference here. When he named the animals, he was giving names which differentiated them from himself. Now he gives a title, 'Woman' (*Isshah* in Hebrew) which is as close as possible to his own title 'Man' (*Ish* in Hebrew). He names her, not as an authority giving a label to a lower creature, but as one who is delighted to find a being who is like himself. It is the new name, the secret name which a lover may give to the loved one, however many names she or he may already possess.

*

Therefore a man leaves his father and mother and clings to his wife, and they become one flesh.

Genesis 2:24

Suddenly we move from a story told in the past tense to a statement very much in the present tense. We realize that the story has not been told merely to give us information about an event in the distant past but to give guidelines concerning our relationships in the immediate present. The man is to detach himself from his parents and identify himself with his wife. She is to be his security and his stability.

This is a remarkable announcement. The community that generated this section of Genesis was a highly patriarchal society, a past-looking, parent-centred, male-dominated, ancestor-honouring polygamous culture where the wife rarely had much personal identity. Normally a woman had to leave home, and was passed from one male controller to another – from father to husband. Her destiny was to be part of the household of her husband's father. Woman was a commodity. Her transfer had to be paid for. In Britain, until recently, the bride was 'given away' – put by her male parent into the hand of the male priest and transferred by him into the hand of the male bridegroom. The ring, given by the bridegroom to the bride, was the last vestige of the bride-price, payable by the bridegroom. Of course, we did our best to overcome this sense that the woman was a commodity being transferred, but the underlying tradition was there. And all the time, embedded in the most ancient strata of the Hebrew Scriptures, and affirmed by Jesus, there was this contrary vision: that it is the man who moves away from parents and makes a new unit with the woman; it is the man who has to change – he has to grow up and create a new identity with his contemporary, the woman. This does not necessarily suit us. It does not fit with older traditions of Africa or Asia or Europe. We are told, sometimes, that we should not expect African people to accept European standards in such matters as marriage, and that we must not force our culture upon them. But this vision of marriage is as un-European as it is un-African. Christian obedience demands at least as great a change for Europeans as it does for Africans. Christ is profoundly non-European, as he is also non-African. His calling is a calling for repentance and change for all people. And this can be measured in such a matter as marriage. In these days, we may claim that we do not live in such a male-dominated society as in the past. Patriarchy is out of date, non-PC. But many modern and detribalized people find it very difficult really to leave father and mother, to cease to be ruled by the images and expectations of parents, and to treat their spouse as a genuinely contemporary person. We can still make good use of this text, incorporated into the teaching of Jesus, as part of the scriptural witness at a marriage service.[7]

*

And the man and his wife were both naked, and were not ashamed.

Genesis 2:25

We return to the man and the woman in Genesis for a final comment. They were both naked, without embarrassment or shame. The commentators on this verse sometimes seem to assume that it means that the man and the woman were not conscious of their sexual identity. That sort of consciousness, these commentators say, came only later, with the Fall, and it was because of their lack of such consciousness that they could be naked without shame. Surely this is, in fact, the exact opposite of the truth. The man is saying of the woman, 'This is it – bone of my bone, flesh of my flesh.' My flesh fits hers, she fits mine; she opens for me, I become part of her. The man cannot be saying this without being aware of his sexual identity right down to the root of his being; the woman cannot hear this estimate of herself without being similarly aware of her sexual identity. Even if, in its grammatical form, this great exclamation is in the man's script only, it still makes sense only if it is really mutual. The discovery that another person can be such a complete physical and spiritual counterpart makes a fundamental difference to the whole of life of woman and man. The man and woman are un-covered; so they dis-cover each other. They have no concealment, no masks, no roles. They can just delight in each other. This awareness of sexuality is a powerful cry of praise to the Creator. Admirals and bishops and judges have to remove all their regalia to be dis-covered by their spouses, to recognize and celebrate each other's sexuality. That is one of the supreme blessings which the Creator offers to us. As Adam said, 'Wow' – or, to use the classical language of the Bible, 'Alleluia'.

For Reflection

This chapter has been largely about language. The man has been called by God to be a symbol-maker. He finds different words to express himself, and to give labels to the things which he encounters. We have noted also, in the previous chapter, the value of being able to live with more than one language, to be able to refer to things with different sets of terms, to have alternative spectacles to see through. We see how language almost breaks down when some wonderful new thing happens – or, indeed, when something terrible happens. In the grounds of St Asaph Cathedral, in North Wales, there is a unique monument; it celebrates the work of a series of men who translated the Bible into Welsh. It is a good place for reflecting on your own use of language, and on the wonder of human communication.

You are yourself a creator of language. Think of the last

thing you said. The chances are that you have never before spoken that exact form of words; the chances also are that no one has taught you to speak it. And think about your own way of speaking about, and of speaking to, your spouse or partner or someone close to you. You can, of course, think about this sort of thing without going specifically to St Asaph. But it is good to reflect on how the Bible has come to you in your language, and then to feel something of the wider marvel of communication.

Questions for Working Groups

For these questions, it would be best to work in small teams of not more than four people, so that you can talk openly and personally with each other.

1. We see with our language. How far do you feel that you have been labelled or misunderstood by the words that have been used to describe you – as 'male' or 'female', 'working class', a 'problem', an 'intellec-tual', 'disabled', or whatever? How do you work with God in using language creatively, without using it to put other people down?

2. What do you think of Adam's cry of delight as he sees the woman? For you, does it seem to be just part of a male-dominated culture? How would you like to see this story re-written, to express what you feel to be important about our relationships? Can you develop an enlarged or alternative version?

7

Searching

Now we have the start of a real living story. Because of its power and imaginative appeal, we need to take care that we receive it in the most helpful way. We can receive it in the same way as we receive such a story as Christ's parable of the prodigal son. The proper question to ask is not so much 'What does this tell us about the distant past?' as 'What does this say about ourselves?' This is not an account of the predicament of the first human beings so much as an account of the predicament of me.

This is the purpose of myth; it is one way of communicating truth. For all communication, there must be some sort of code; the most bare literal facts are communicated in one sort of code. Myth is another sort of code. It is the statement of spiritual truth by means of a story set in the natural world. About any myth, we have to ask whether it conveys something which we can recognize as true, about ourselves and about what we know about God, or (and this is perfectly possible) whether it conveys something which is fundamentally and dangerously untrue. If it is a myth which does its job, it will convey something more than could be conveyed by a prose translation or by an exposition of the theory lying behind it. It will be like a piece of music or a painting, untranslatable into another medium. For me, the art of ballet is a blind spot; but I can appreciate the answer of a dancer who was asked about the meaning of a particular dance, and answered, 'If I could put it into words, I wouldn't bother to dance it.' Beethoven, we are told, was asked for an interpretation of a sonata which he had played, and responded simply by playing it again. Whether or not that story is strictly historical, I don't know, but it is a good specimen of a myth. During the twentieth century, some prominent theologians argued that the biblical 'myths' arose out of an environment so different from our own that we needed to 'de-mythologize' them; we needed to cut away the story element and just accept the core meaning. The best comment I have heard about this was from a Pentecostal friend, a man who believed in the literal accuracy of the whole Bible. He was actually talking about the healing miracles of Jesus, but his approach could be applied to the whole biblical narrative. He said, 'I would agree entirely that we need to demythologize these stories. And how? By stopping thinking about them as past history and seeing that they are happening today. Then they cease to be *only* myths and become saving truth about us now.'

Whether we are conscious of them or not, we are living with myths all the time. Such a myth has a root in the natural world, and in our language about the natural world. But there is also a meaning – perhaps a whole bundle of meanings – which we recognize as being conveyed by the myth. Take the symbol of 'Jordan'. It is located, in geographical terms, as a river running from north to south in the Middle East. It is located in history as the boundary which the people of Israel had to cross to enter the promised land. From this it becomes the 'Jordan' of our individual pilgrimage which we anticipate when, whether at Cardiff Arms Park or a wedding or wherever, we sing Williams Pantycelyn's line 'When I tread the verge of Jordan ...'; we are transferring the meaning to our own death. Further, 'Jordan' is the water in which, following Jesus, we are baptized. Then there is the vast political significance of Jordan for communities – Arab, Jew,

Christian, Muslim, Israeli, Palestinian – of the contemporary Middle East. There is also the significance cunningly hidden in those freedom songs which have been called Negro Spirituals – 'Deep River, my home is over Jordan, Deep River, Lord.' For the slave in the Southern States, 'Jordan' was the Ohio, the boundary between the slave-states and the free. This is perhaps closest to the meaning that 'Jordan' would have for those communities of the Bible who were most conscious of either their past circumstances as slaves or their present circumstances as exiles. In a world where there are still so many slaves, what can this old symbol, or myth, of 'Jordan' mean for us, in song or prayer?

However, this story is not just a timeless parable. It is about the beginnings. It is rightly in the text called *Genesis*. We can never know much about the individual lives of our distant ancestors. Even animals with complex brains cannot think or reflect in the way that humans can. At some stage in the evolution of human life, something started to happen which we call thought or reflection. At some stage, a being appeared who was capable of this sort of thought, whose parents had not been capable. At some stage, a being appeared who was capable of making decisions about right and wrong, who could make moral choices, who could therefore consciously decide in favour of wrong. That being would be the first who would morally be entitled to be called 'human'. The first couple whose moral ability could be passed on to their offspring would be the first human couple. This story gives them names: Eve and Adam. We could think of these new beginnings as mental or moral or spiritual mutations; they do not necessarily have any connection with the kinds of mutation that can be traced by way of the physical evidences that can be recovered from the past. It is difficult to imagine such developments. But some such new beginnings must have happened, at some point. And the universe has never been the same since that day.

These stories are told as stories, not as theories. If we divide people into storytellers and theory-builders, Hebrews come down firmly on the side of storytellers. Jesus was a Hebrew, a storyteller; Paul, a Greek-thinking man with a Hebrew education, was more of a theory-builder. The Hebrew Scriptures do not build any kind of theory on the basis of the Genesis stories; they do not lay down a doctrine of 'the Fall'. They do not offer these stories as an explanation of the origin of evil. The stories witness to the character of evil as we experience it in the present, in its strange way of working through good things such as the tree, the woman, the man, the snake, the good creatures of God.

Evil is not described as a creation of God. Nor is it seen as an equal and opposite force to good. Evil just happens, through human choice. There is no observed mechanism. It's not as if there was a devil to come in from outside the scene to carry the blame; that would lead us away from experience into a whole range of theory-building. Even the concept of evil is not there. Evil things simply happen; and they bring a curse.

*

Now the serpent was more crafty than any other wild animal that the Lord God had made. He said to the woman,

> *'Did God say, "You shall not eat from any tree in the garden"?'*

The woman said to the serpent,

> *'We may eat of the fruit of the trees in the garden; but God said, "You shall not eat of the fruit of the tree that is in the middle of the garden, nor shall you touch it, or you shall die."'*

But the serpent said to the woman,

> *'You will not die; for God knows that when you eat of*

it your eyes will be opened, and you will be like God,
knowing good and evil.'
So when the woman saw that the tree was good for food,
and that it was a delight to the eyes, and that the tree was
to be desired to make one wise, she took of its fruit and
ate; and she also gave some to her husband, who was
with her, and he ate. Then the eyes of both were opened,
and they knew that they were naked; and they sewed fig
leaves together and made loincloths for themselves.

They heard the sound of the Lord God walking in the
garden at the time of the evening breeze, and the man and
his wife hid themselves from the presence of the Lord
God among the trees of the garden. But the Lord God
called to the man, and said to him,

'Where are you?'
He said,

'I heard the sound of you in the garden, and I was
afraid because I was naked, and I hid myself.'
He said,

'Who told you that you were naked? Have you eaten
from the tree of which I commanded you not to eat?'
The man said,

'The woman whom you gave to be with me, she gave
me fruit from the tree and I ate.'
Then the Lord God said to the woman,

'What is this that you have done?'
The woman said,

'The serpent tricked me and I ate.'

Genesis 3:1–13

Enter the snake. May we be very naïve and ask, 'Why a
snake?' The characters that we have met so far – the man,
the woman, the tree – have been universal and central to

human experience. But even in Africa most people do not meet snakes every day. Concerning verses 14 to 19 of this chapter of Genesis, commentators tell us that the story is recorded to explain the origin of some familiar features of our world. This makes sense with regard to such matters as the pain of childbirth, the need for hard work, and the certainty of death. But this theory implies that we need an explanation of the snake's method of travel as much as we need an explanation of the pains of childbirth. Why the great interest in the snake? Why not a question about cattle or disease or rainfall or a dozen things which are more central to human experience than the snake's method of locomotion?

We cannot get away from the strange fascination which snakes seem to have for our human imagination. In the Bible, they are poisonous dangers; but they are also sources of healing. Around the throne of God the seraphim fly; they are the angelic, winged serpents that form the highest of the nine orders of heavenly beings. The image of the snake was at the centre of idolatrous worship; it was also a forecast of the crucified Christ who would be lifted up for the healing of the world.[1] Elsewhere, the snake can be a symbol of immortality, a female symbol or a phallic symbol. The snake attracts legends to itself, even among people who have never had to deal with them. People credit them with extraordinary speed, although the fastest of them moves only at a human walking-pace. Snake-charmers still can get an audience at fairs. There is a large area on the banks of the Teifi which is sealed off from the public because it is home to some adders. In popular symbolism, we have a traditional children's game; the significance of 'ladders' for ascending is obvious; but why 'snakes' for the descent? One child that I asked said that it is because snakes are slimy. Are they? How has he got that idea?

So there may be a good reason for the prominence of the

snake in the story. It would seem that the snake is one of the most complex symbols in our human imagination. It can stand for a real mix-up of ideas. In one symbol, it can stand for the mixed nature of 'good and evil' which we experience as a bind, as an inhibition on our ability to make choices. Like the cross, it can stand for the best and the worst. We don't know what to make of the snake; we don't know what to make of ourselves.

The snake in Genesis chapter 3 is not the Devil. Its characteristic is not wickedness but subtlety or cunning. It wants to have an informed discussion about God. This is the task of theology. The snake is the first theologian. It is in business to raise questions about God, to make sure that people will give their best attention to ultimate issues. Its duty is to ensure that such issues are expressed and faced, for an unbelief which is repressed can be more dangerous than any conscious doubt. The question is not a matter of abstract speculation. It is quite specific. 'Did God say "You shall not eat of any tree of the garden"?'

The snake tries to analyse the nature of God. Is a particular word the sort of thing that God says? Does this word fit in to what we think we know about him? This is the stock-in-trade of theology. We make God a subject of study. We try to understand the one who stands over us. We try to explain him, to make him clear, so one human creature can exchange words about God with another. One person gets a first-class degree in theology and another fails. The knowledge of God becomes a subject of competition like geology or archery; it becomes a commodity which some people can accumulate.

Isaiah puts the theologian's question back where it belongs: '"To whom, then, will you liken me, whom set up as my equal?", asks the Holy One.'[2] How can you know the sort of thing that God says? The servant of God is not the person who conducts the best discussion about God but the one who has heard the word of God and holds to it. It is *doing* the Sermon on the Mount, not the interpreting of it, that is required.[3] There is only one important question which has to be put against any theological discussion, whether at the level of a house-group in a little parish or of a university seminar: 'Is this discussion leading us to greater obedience to the purpose of the Kingdom of God in God's world?' We should test every study-group meeting by this standard, and every theological lecture.

The cunning snake approaches the woman. She is easier than the man to engage in discussion, not because she is female but because she has heard of God's prohibition only by hearsay. The snake offers an idea of God which is incorrect and can easily be knocked down. It suggests that God might have forbidden the eating of the fruit of all the trees. The woman has been informed correctly, so she puts herself on the side of the truth. She states that the snake's suggestion is wrong. God has allowed them to eat the fruit of all the trees, except for the one in the middle. So far, so good. But she is attracted by the idea of making the prohibition more severe than it really is. She elaborates the prohibition by claiming that not only eating but also touching is forbidden. An ogre-god is beginning to appear in her answer. She needs an authority-figure to resent, and she begins to develop grounds for complaint. She makes herself into a candidate for the snake's sympathy. The only proper and necessary answer to the snake's question would have been a straight 'No'. But this would have been too simple a response to the sophisticated snake. So she allows untruth to obtain a small foothold in her. By an apparently insignificant exaggeration she has lost something of her integrity. She has shown that she is vulnerable to false suggestion. The snake takes advantage, and moves in with a direct attack.

The snake states baldly that what God has said is not

true. 'God', says the snake, 'is pretending to protect you from death by preventing you from eating that fruit. But God is not interested in your well-being; he wants to protect himself. He is scared that you will become a rival to himself.' The snake tries to bring the Lord God down to the level of the tribal gods of the nations around, who were often motivated by envy of each other. A snake like this, which talks and tempts, is indeed an alien intrusion into the world-view of the Hebrews. They would probably see it as an importation from paganism. For them, it would stand for all that they had been delivered from, in their hard journey out of slavery. It is the idolatrous authorities of injustice and untruth who behave like this snake. Let us be warned.

'You will be like God' is the snake's promise. How can this be? God has made the human beings, so how can they make themselves to be like their maker? The answer is only if 'God' can mean something other than the God who makes us and has authority over us – only if 'God' can be something that we design. There can be both the God who makes us, who forms us in his own image and likeness, and a god in our own minds, which we can imitate by our own exertions. The Hebrews knew all about this second kind of god. They were surrounded by communities that prided themselves on their idols. Idolatry, for the Hebrews, was a much more serious danger than atheism. Idolatry was not just an insult to the one true God; idolatry leads directly to the break-up of the human community. Your idol stands for you and takes your side; my idol stands for me and takes my side. Both of us will sacrifice generously to our idols, so as to persuade them to succeed on our behalf. So the realm of gods becomes a powerful source of death and destruction, of competitiveness and injustice. It does not matter very much whether the idol is an elaborate carving or an expensive motor car, an area of land seized from an enemy or a successful financial project, a dream home or an acclaimed intellectual achievement. Like the golden calf, it will be something that we have made, achieved by our own energies.[4] It will open our eyes, so that we see our environment in its terms. It will shape our understanding of good and evil according to its priorities. It will deny that the earth is the Lord's, and will encourage its devotees to see the whole of creation as units of merchandise. That is what idolatry is about. The Hebrew people knew themselves as people delivered from the rule of idolatry through being delivered from the rule of slave-owners. The snake's persuasion would take them back down that road.

The woman's attention has been drawn to prohibitions and possibilities which make her feel incomplete and inadequate, dissatisfied with herself as a creation of a good God. She allows herself to be defined by the way in which the snake defines her. She allows someone else to tell her who she is and what she should be wanting. She is attracted by the possibility of getting a status for herself by grasping, rather than resting in the greater identity which she has already been given by the creative energy of God. As well as being the first theologian, the snake is the first advertiser, the first spin-doctor, the first agent of consumerism.

The snake is not much to blame. All it did was to raise questions and arguments, which could have been disposed of quite quickly. It makes a couple of utterances and then is silent. The woman is not swept off her feet. She ponders, exercising both imagination and intellect. She allows herself to become aware of a whole range of considerations which make the fruit attractive to her. They all combine to make her feel incomplete and inadequate. She needs something to compensate her for this feeling of inadequacy. There is no shortage of food for her; but she will feel deprived unless she has *this* food. The tree is beautiful to look at; but this is not enough. She cannot tolerate it being just a beautiful thing outside herself. It makes her feel a lack of beauty in herself. It makes her feel insecure about her own wisdom; she has to get it for herself, to make herself wise. She needs to contemplate it, to absorb it intellectually, to have a mastery over it. She must possess it. She must consume it. She acts in accordance with a *felt* insecurity instead of in accordance with a *known* security. This, in a word, is faithlessness. It is the root of sin, because it is a refusal of what the Creator gives. It is the ambition to be independent of God. It can lead, logically, to an ambition to be independent of nature – see the treeless landscapes and animal-less machines which form the environment of so much sci-fi fantasy.

Here is another point where we can learn from the differences between this earlier story of creation, in Genesis 2 and 3, and the later one, in Genesis 1. Chapter 1 does, broadly speaking, fit in with the biological fact that the human being represents the ascent of the evolutionary process to its highest point. Chapter 3 tells of the cultural or moral fact that something has gone wrong. We could not have this sense of wrongness if we had not developed to a level where moral consciousness became possible. Only a being which can consciously be in relationship with God can decide not to be in relationship with God. So, evil is not a throwback to our primitive past. It is not a relic of our animal nature, which we might hope to grow out of. It is a product of our advanced nature. The faculties of rational thought and verbal communication give humans their most distinctive mastery over other species; but it is precisely those faculties which give rise to the dangers which threaten us all with extinction. No doubt a lot of advanced scientific skill went into the organization of the Holocaust; but physical violence is the product of spiritual violence, and without the spiritual motive there would have been no Holocaust.

Humans have developed to a level where it can make sense to accuse a human being of being inhuman, whereas it does not make sense to accuse a rat of being unratty. The behaviour of the woman and man in our story is inhuman, insofar as it disregards a primary characteristic of the design of a human being, namely, our being made to be in bonded relationship with God. This is a moral or cultural aspect of what it means to be human. We have survived to become *physically* human. Now we can be *morally* human, even if this conflicts with the demands of survival. We are free to insist that righteousness remains righteousness even if it does not triumph. We are free to assert that the virtue of forgiveness is of supreme value even if it is completely opposed to the instinct for survival. In fact, that great pioneer of evolutionary biology, Thomas Huxley, went so far as to state: 'The ethical progress of society depends not on imitating the cosmic process, still less on running away from it, but on combating it.'[5]

The woman accepts the snake's advice: she takes and eats. She shares with her husband, and he eats. We cannot put a label on their offence, thus classifying it as the breaking of a law, or as an example of pride or greed or any other generalization. We cannot construct a universal law based on the instruction that the woman and the man disregarded. The whole story is not much use as a moral example. Sin, here, is not the infringement of a law. It is a specific action, which is sinful because, in order to commit it, they change their priorities and act as if their relatedness to God is not the primary truth about themselves. This story is truly about us; it is about the motives and the mistakes which can corrupt our relationships every day.

The snake was right; the man and the woman do not face an immediate death penalty. Their eyes are indeed opened. But the knowledge which results is not what they expected. They become aware of their nakedness. Nakedness had been a blessing; now it becomes an embarrassment. The Hebrews were particularly sensitive about nakedness. Roman cruelty decreed that criminals should be crucified completely naked, and this was one of the reasons why this method of execution was so hated. Most Christian art insists on a loincloth; we can't face the reality, either. Shame enters the Genesis story; it is a means to protect us from full knowledge of each other. The story, again, does not give us a worked-out theory; it simply states that the unhindered consciousness of sexual difference is part of the blessedness of creation, and that man and woman who are revolting against their created blessedness discover that that they cannot cope with this consciousness. The coverings which the man and the woman devise for themselves have to be removed for the sex act, which the Hebrews called 'knowing' the other person. The man and the woman know that something has gone wrong, and they are preparing to make accusations about who is responsible. They no longer can afford fully to know each other; so they have to disguise the differences between them. They make aprons out of the largest leaves which are available to them. Wearing them, the man and woman unite themselves to each other in a new unconstructive way; their union is no longer the coming together of two complementaries, but the ganging-up of two insecure culprits in fear of authority.

Again, this is not a theory about sex or shame or sin. It is a story which portrays one of the commonest puzzles of life, namely that an apparently reasonable action can lead to misery and a destruction of a most precious relationship. There was nothing wrong with the eating of the fruit, except that they knew that God did not want it to happen. Otherwise it was entirely reasonable. It is this kind of snarl-up which causes more disappointment and resentment than almost anything else; even now, I doubt whether there is a word which can be used to describe such a confused experience.

Let me summarize the process. The man and woman treat the relationship with God as being of secondary importance to the satisfying of immediate lusts and the hunger for self-made achievement. God's interests are despised and rejected; the man and woman suddenly feel exposed and unmasked when they realize that they will have to meet this despised God. There is nothing that they can do to rectify the situation – they cannot put the clock back – so they take a ridiculously ineffective action to try to disguise their sense that something is dangerously wrong. They meet God; and finally God acts as the only one who is still free to act, and makes it possible for them to appear before him. This is not a theological generalization; the story could not have been shaped in this way unless it had been based on human experience. In the above summary, for the terms 'God' and 'the man and woman', substitute 'my partner' and 'me', or 'Margaret' and 'Tom', and see how it works. Evidently, the authors of this chapter felt that this sort of experience is so central to real life that a representative version of it was needed at the very start of the story of the relationship between God and human beings.

In Genesis, we see these issues portrayed in the story of representative individuals. But they are equally to be found in churches, nations and political groups – all kinds of communities. In the days of Jesus, the Jewish people had an opportunity to grow into a wider definition of themselves than they were willing to accept. Jesus behaved as a leader who would include, in one community, sinners and prostitutes, collaborators and nationalists, outsiders and gentiles, the poor, the disabled and the children.[6] But when he came to the nation's cultural centre, he found that the city was unable to accept the kind of peace that he was offering, and this moved him to tears.[7] We Gentiles owe our place within the Christian movement to the steady struggle of the followers of Jesus to create a community which would be as inclusive as Jesus intended (see the whole story of Acts). But the sin of the Church is, fundamentally, the same as the sin of old Israel and the sin of Eve: we prefer to trust in the narrow range of what we know and can grasp and control, rather than in what God is offering and has in store for us.

When people or groups disguise their differences, as the woman and the man do in this story, it may well be because, consciously or unconsciously, they are finding a common enemy in God. According to Luke, the common desire to get rid of Jesus made friends of those two most different people: Pilate and Herod. Mark tells of the ganging-up of two unlikely allies – the Pharisees and the Herodians – for a similar purpose. John describes an even stranger collaboration of disciple, foreign soldiers, servants of the religious establishment and representatives of a movement for moral revival, in a joint enterprise for the arresting of the truth.[8] We do want to work and pray for the reunion of the Church, and for unity within our society. But we need to beware of thinking that any old unity is the supreme goal. We may find ourselves ganging-up against the truth, or squeezing out the poorest and the voiceless, whose interests can most easily be ignored. We may find ourselves united by a dislike of diversity, or a desire to suppress the inconvenient or the awkward, and so exclude part of the Creator's blessings. We may find ourselves united by a common fear of the world around. We could unite in order to be a better opponent of the world instead of a better servant of the world. The mere overlooking of the differences between a half-dozen conformist and unrepentant churches would be an ecumenical disaster. We do believe that God wants us to receive his precious gift of unity, but he will withhold it until the Christian movement has such a concern for his world that it can use the gift rightly.

All through the story, this is God's world. God is master of it; it is his home. He walks in the garden as of right. The world is not only God's work-place; it is also his place of leisure. He is not a commuting God, going back to heaven at knocking-off time. He shares the evening breeze with us, as well as the midday heat.

Are you happy with such a God? For the most part, we would prefer not to have to sing 'The earth is the Lord's'. We behave as if it is for us to carve up among ourselves and claim it as our own fragmented property. The sound of God walking among us will be the last thing that we want to hear. Keep God in church! Then we will know where we can be safe. Certainly, there are special places set aside to be the methods of his presence. Sacraments and church buildings and Sunday and Bible study are part of God's kindness to us; but they can also serve as 'trees' by which we hide from him as he walks in his world. Nearly 50 years on, I can still remember the remark of a man who was passionately committed to social justice and had conscientiously avoided having anything to do with churches and clergy; his testimony to 'conversion' was, 'I feel now that my home is part of God's world'[9] (he was, incidentally, the same Trade Union member whom I mentioned in the previous chapter, who felt that, as a Christian, his duty was to be at the Union meeting on Sunday).

The man and woman flee because they cannot stand before God; they use these good things of creation – the trees – as a means of concealment. What is given as a source of nourishment is taken as a hiding-place. The things of this world are supposed to be a means of community between us and God, but they cannot decide for themselves; we can decide whether to use them for good or evil.

By his presence, God stimulates guilt. But that is not his primary intention or his nature. The Church, in its various forms and traditions, has been extremely successful at increasing the amount of guilt in the world; like some other institutions, it knows that if you can keep people feeling guilty, you can control them. The story of Adam and Eve has, itself, been one of the instruments for this process. But insofar as the Church has been true to the ministry of Jesus, this has not been its primary intention. Jesus got into considerable trouble by encouraging and accepting people who were supposed to feel guilty, and by tussling with people who were trying to hide from their guilt. Just as the enemy of faith is not doubt but the repression of doubt, so the enemy of grace is not guilt but the repression of guilt. His aim was not to increase guilt, but to bring it to the surface and get rid of it.[10]

So far, we have had a command in the mouth of God, and a statement. Now we have God's first question. It too is typical. 'Where are you?' It seems that God is ignorant and has to make enquiries.

We humans can make God a searcher. God does not know in advance everywhere we shall go or everything we shall get up to. He watches to see how his creation is going to work out. We humans have developed into creatures with uniquely large brains; that gives us choices and responsibilities such as no other creature has. We also have a unique ability to place our thumb opposite our fingers: we can use our hands to receive gifts, and to grasp and grab. God watches to see how we shall choose. This is part of God's nature. God's authority is not the authority of one who has nothing to learn, but the authority of an eternal searcher. If there were a fixed number of things to know, then it would make sense to say that God knows them all. But as the universe develops and as human history unfolds, there are always new things to know. Jesus was a teacher because he was all the time a learner, a continual questioner. The Church, as a teacher, is called similarly to be a learner. It will discover things in this century which it did not know in the previous one. In doing so, it will reflect something of the character of God. God, in the Hebrew

Scriptures, is not the static, uninfluenced one that is
worshipped in some other traditions. God has feelings;
God is able to change his mind, to adapt to new situations.
God is able to be influenced. A being who cannot be
influenced must be more like a mineral thing, towards the
bottom of the cosmic order. The supreme one is one who
indeed can be influenced, can be responsive and so be
unpredictable. So we can claim that God is abundantly
compassionate. This does not diminish God's authority.
Rather, it proclaims him to be the source of all spiritual
energy. He, the Creator, feels the anxiety before the
creature does; this is the reason for his question.

God is the searcher. He does not necessarily know where
we are going. But he remains God. He will not stop searching. It is impossible to escape from God. The Hebrews'
picture of the universe was not in accordance with our
scientific cosmology. They thought of the universe as a
three-layer sandwich of heaven and earth and underworld.
But this did not overrule their deepest insights about God.
Psalm 139 powerfully insists that, whatever one's picture of
the universe may be, God will be everywhere in it; he will
not be restricted to a special divine neighbourhood. The
book of Jonah tells of the impossibility of escaping from
God and from God's calling. In both the Psalm and in
Jonah, God is the constant knower. He knows how we are
made. He has been watching over our growth and our reac-
tions. He knows, not because he is a spy or Big Brother; he
knows in the way that a painter knows his picture, in the
way that a novelist or dramatist knows her characters. So
we can trust God's knowing of us. It is not a knowing
which is in business to catch us out or to make us be something which we are not. It is not the superior, powerful kind
of knowing which is claimed by the person who insists on
telling us, 'Oh, I know exactly how you feel!' It is not the
intimidating kind of claim to which the black preacher

Howard Thurman (long before Martin Luther King) made the entirely proper reply: 'When the Southern white person says, " I understand the Negro", what he really means is that he has a knowledge of the Negro within the limitations of the boundaries which the white man has set up. The kind of Negro he understands has no existence except in his own mind.'[11] A person who feels that they are known in this sort of way has every right to try to be unknowable, to behave irresponsibly or unpredictably; otherwise they will become a slave of the other person's knowledge. But God's way of knowing is the knowing of one who knows our potential, and who judges us by how far we let ourselves grow into the potential for which he has designed us.

The man and the woman know this. They know that God is God. If he were not, there would be no need to flee. But the fleeing is useless, and they realize this as soon as they hear the question. God is the one who draws us out of our silence and isolation. God asks us the question with such authority that we have to do something about it. This was the basic miracle of Christ, not that he did this or that, but that he was *there,* available, meeting people, wearing a garment with a hem that could be touched.[12] And that is how the Church, as the Body of Christ, is supposed to be, wherever it is located. Its inescapable 'being there' comes before all the details of its programme. If it tries to act by coercion rather than by persuasion, if it represents God's grace as absolute force rather than as patient love, it will misrepresent the God whose first word to man and woman is this searching question.

Up to this point, the man has been able to make appropriate answers to questions and opportunities. He has named animals; he has been ecstatic at the sight of the woman. But now his responses go awry. God's question has been simply, 'Where are you?' The man hears the question as, 'Why have you been hiding?' God sends out a message of friendly enquiry; the man receives the message as if it is coming from an accusing authority. It is not God's speaking that has gone wrong; it is the man's hearing equipment which has become distorted. It filters off part of God's message and inserts other meanings which were not intended. Again, this sort of distortion of communication is a common human experience, typical of how we mis-hear each other; our story tells us that it happened in the first conversation between God and the human creation.

The question 'Where are you?' need not be an accusation. It can be neutral; it can be caring and loving. But Adam is anxious. He has not been behaving as a guest on God's land; he is improperly dressed, and he hears the question as a threat. Jesus picks up this theme in his parable about the wedding garment.[13] Commentators note that it would be unreasonable to expect a man picked up off the street to be spruced up in a morning-suit ready for a wedding, and therefore suggest that Matthew has rather roughly tacked two independent parables together. This may be correct; but, thanks to this editorial device, we do have the two parables following on from each other. The question, 'My *friend*, how did you get in here without a wedding garment?', is not necessarily a loaded or threatening one. The man has a perfectly good reason: he has been invited off the street and has had no chance to get himself ready. But the man gags himself; he refuses to speak. He refuses to acknowledge that he is there only at the king's invitation; he refuses the role of a guest. This is tantamount to claiming a right to be there on his own terms. It is because of this silence, not because of his inappropriate clothing, that he is thrown out. The message here, therefore, is the same as that of the previous part of the parable, where the guests who had been invited renounced their role as guests, and chose rather to give priority to things on which they had rights – the commodities that they had got for themselves, such as land and animals and women. They preferred this self-organized independence to the dependent role of being guests.

The more clothed we become – the more we dress up in properties and status and degrees and businesses and religious convictions and what-not – the harder it becomes for us simply to meet as persons; the harder it becomes for us to meet God. The Christian gospel tells us that God overcame the disadvantage of having the supreme status of all, the status of being God; he was seen at his most godlike in the person of one who had no property, nowhere to lay his head, and ended up totally naked on a cross.

The man starts to live according to his knowledge of good and evil. He starts to organize his own justification. This means that he abandons his most precious relationships, in order to allocate blame. The woman is to blame. The woman *whom you gave me* is to blame, so you are to blame. The woman becomes an enemy, and God becomes an enemy. Where is the previous joy in the existence of the woman? Where is the previous relationship of trust in God as the host? Destroyed, as the man tries to prove that he is in the right. His statements are correct, but they are arguments of death. The eating has indeed led to death, the death of the relationship and security for which he was designed.

Previously, the story has spoken of 'wife' and 'husband'. But these words do not apply now. The man finds it impossible to say, 'It's my wife's fault.' He denies the relationship. He refers to her not as 'this wife of mine' but as 'the woman whom you gave me'. Again, we find the same process in the parables of Jesus. The elder son cannot bring himself to call his junior 'this brother of mine'; he refers to him as 'this son of yours'. By doing so, he disowns his relationship with his father as well as with his brother. It is impossible to disown the human brother without disowning the God who has

118   *God at Work*

given us this brother. And there is another crippling motive shared by the two brothers. The younger brother, far away in trouble, decides to opt for the role of slave. He wants to cease to be a son, to earn his place in the household. He carefully rehearses his speech to announce this policy. But (and this 'but' is a key moment in the story) the father takes no notice of this well-prepared 'confession'. He immediately takes steps to clothe the son in the appropriate garments and to express in every possible way his son's status as a son. When the elder brother hears of this, he also opts for a slave-state. He insists on having earned his place. He emphasizes his own claim and his brother's blame. He refuses to accept the fact that he, like his brother, owes his place in the household to his father's love. The sharp edge of Jesus' story is this: the younger son's place in the household is secure; what about the elder son? Will he or won't he join the party? The story is left unfinished. It should be printed with a long row of dots after the last sentence. Are the Pharisees and scribes, for whom the parable was told, going to join Jesus' party with tax-collectors and sinners? Or are they going to claim their status, and thus confine themselves to a state of slavery? And what about the congregation of honest Christians who hear the parable read to them on Sunday morning? Where does it leave us? We also need to hear the story with a long row of dots at the end. We also have to fill in the conclusion on our own behalf.[14]

The woman follows the same technique as the man. She accuses the snake. In so doing, she accuses the snake's maker. Her statement may be accurate, but it is offered not as a way of seeking the truth but as a way of finding someone to blame. She does not stop to ask, 'What good does it do to say this?' The snake, after all, did very little. It merely started a speculative conversation.

I'm not to blame. I don't take responsibility for what has happened. I was just carrying out orders. I don't have a mind of my own. I am merely a slave. I am just a victim. I do not have freedom, and I do not want to claim freedom, because that would mean that I am responsible. The Hebrew Scriptures, especially in the prophets, are largely about God's calling of his people to take responsibility for themselves, to reject the attractiveness of a return to slavery, to behave as true adults. Many of the psalms celebrate the freedom of those who are in a responsible relationship with God. In the Gospels, we see the difference that Jesus made – people were carrying the beds that previously had carried them, people accepted responsibility for their actions, people stood up against authorities which would have kept them disabled.[15] Jesus was not a tree to hide behind. His Church is not supposed to be a tree to hide behind, either. All around us there are voices which tell us that such things as Third World debt, or the crisis in the Middle East, or racism in our cities, or the poor condition of our transport, are not our problems. The effect of the Christian movement in the world should be that people really do take responsibility, not just for the well-being of the Church, but for the health of creation. In its local form, that is what the Church is all about.

The woman and the man both set themselves up as prosecuting counsels. We play this role with greatest vigour when we ourselves are most afraid of finding ourselves in the role of defendant. We seek a status of acceptability for ourselves, not by seeking reconciliation but by finding a greater degree of unacceptability in persons who are different from ourselves. We can identify evil as something which can easily be recognized in ... whoever we most dislike: journalists, economists, Communists, pedestrians, young people, sexual minorities, blacks, whites, Muslims, nationalists, evangelicals, or whatever. This becomes good news. Religion can be an attractive instrument for telling us who is to blame. A religion that does not clearly tell us whom we should disapprove of is not likely to be very successful. The only solution will be if someone is willing to be the victim of our prosecution, to be reckoned with the transgressors, and so pull out into consciousness the latent guilt which makes us so keen to establish our innocence. And that, we believe, is the policy of God in Christ.

So we should not see this story as an account of the origin of evil, as something that happened long ago and far away. If we could identify evil in this way, it would not be evil as we know it; it would only be fate, an inevitable process about which we can do nothing. The sin of the man and the woman is not the cause of our sin. The purpose of the story is not to tell us whom to blame. The point of the story is to show how useless it is to look for such a solution. The story is, in a true and important sense, myth. It is about the past, certainly, because humanity is in the past; we are not the first people to whom these things happen. But the story is primarily about us. When we hear the word in the story, 'Adam, where are you?', we hear God speaking directly to us.

For Reflection

One of the exercises that trainee actors have to practise is to take a simple sentence – such as 'Lend me that pen' – and say it over and over with many different ways of expression and accenting, many different moods and feelings. Try doing this – aloud – with the simple words, 'Where are you?' Feel the meaning of it in as many different ways as you can.

Go into a wood, with another person, and try to be like children, hiding behind trees. What does it feel like? Is it, for you, just a childlike and innocent experience? Or does it bring up memories of a refusal to accept responsibility, a dodging away from some sort of reality?

Questions for Working Groups

1. There are four characters in this story for you to identify with. Your group can split into four teams, to look at the story from the point of view of the snake, the man, the woman, and God. In your role and character, what are you wanting? What are you hoping for and aiming at? What are your feelings as the story progresses? Meet each other and exchange your impressions.

2. How do you see the parable of the prodigal son, with reference to your local church? Who is/are the elder son? Who is going to join the party – or not join the party?

3. Do you feel that we are in a culture where there seems to be a lot of enthusiasm for finding people to blame? Why is this? What does your church contribute – does it encourage people to blame others, or does it encourage us to take responsibility ourselves?

8

Making a New Beginning

The Lord God said to the serpent,
 'Because you have done this, cursed are you among all animals and among all wild creatures; upon your belly you shall go, and dust shall you eat all the days of your life. I will put enmity between you and the woman, and between your offspring and hers; he will strike your head, and you will strike his heel.'
To the woman he said,
 'I will greatly increase your pangs in childbearing; in pain you shall bring forth children, yet your desire shall be for your husband, and he shall rule over you.'
And to the man he said,
 'Because you have listened to the voice of your wife, and have eaten of the tree about which I commanded you, "You shall not eat of it," cursed is the ground because of you; in toil you shall eat of it all the days of your life; thorns and thistles it shall bring forth for you; and you shall eat the plants of the field. By the sweat of your face you shall eat bread until you return to the ground, for out of it you were taken; you are dust, and to dust you shall return.'

Genesis 3:14–19

God the Creator is also God the Judge. He passes sentence.

There is a curse upon the snake. In a literal sense, what is said to the snake would really be more appropriate to a worm. Snakes do not literally eat earth. But the snake represents the danger of religious chatter and speculation. It is unfruitful. It slithers around, sniping away at people's honest desire to find God and to work with God. It is a threat to the man and woman who are simply loved by God. It is a threat to children. Theology which is steered by the figure of Jesus and the search for the kingdom of God's justice is one thing; intellectual spinning of God-gossip is quite another, and that is what the snake represents. It is a special disease of the professionally religious. It gets at the Body of Christ in the heel, furthest from the heart. Evidently there was plenty of this sort of thing in New Testament times.[1] It becomes a game, a hobby, a decoration for people whose lives are reasonably comfortable. It becomes a means of display of cleverness, a tool of dominance and dispossession, to show who is in control. This sort of religious chatter is, therefore, a particularly offensive scandal for people who are being ground into the earth either by personal disaster or by social injustice.

The snake does not have the last word. The offspring of the woman will be vulnerable to the snake's offspring; but the snake's offspring also will be vulnerable to that of the woman. Christian preachers have seen this as a forecast of the gospel of Christ. A new Eve has come, and her son, the new Adam, will overcome the snake. The human being is vulnerable, with a heel which is at the snake's level; but the head of the snake is more vulnerable still. Jesus of Nazareth was a victim of the religious games and political tricks of human beings. But, by allowing himself to be their victim, he drew the sting, and rose from the dead to establish a community of a new Adam.

There are separate words of gloomy prophecy for the woman and the man. Accusation has come between them.

They are separate, at odds with each other, in spite of their feeble attempts to disguise their differences.

For the woman, pleasure and pain, good and evil, exist together. In the first chapter, human reproduction was a simple blessing, like that of other animals. Here, it is also a curse. Man and woman are together, which is still a blessing, but their togetherness involves domination of one by the other, and that is a curse. They will be rivals and enemies of each other, as well as being spouses. Pregnancy is to be a time of anxiety; birth is to be hard work, a moment of great stress for both mother and child. The bearing of children, and the raising of them through childhood and adolescence to adulthood, is to be difficult and hazardous. It is certainly tough, being a human mother; the baby's big brain creates great problems for the mother's pelvic structure ('she walks with a wiggle because her children are so clever'); but we cannot separate the moment of birth from the process of formation into adulthood, which is so much longer with humans than with other species. 'Education, education and education' may be an impressive statement of political priorities, but this seems to apply only when the child becomes old enough to be incorporated into the schooling industry. Mothering (and parenting as a whole) is not reckoned as 'work' – unless one is mothering someone else's child. Yet we all acknowledge that the real work of person-making takes place before the start of formal schooling. Instead, we have one day a year when mothering is honoured. At its worst, this is just sentimental tokenism, an excuse for not taking the work of mothering as a serious part of the fabric of society all year round.

One of the most unprecedented elements in the teaching of Jesus was the way he insisted that children have value *in themselves,* and not merely as future adults. He also insisted on treating women as morally responsible persons, and not as some sort of defective men. Jesus was, therefore, in principle undoing and reversing the curse on the woman in the Genesis story. St Paul is often thought to have had a poor view of women, and indeed of the sex relationship as a whole. But he also addressed women as morally responsible persons, and this was an almost unheard-of idea in those days. He insisted that in Christ's fellowship woman is as essential to man as man is to woman; that must have been a difficult idea for many of his readers. Certainly, there are times when Paul seems to have conformed to the expectations of his culture; but there were other times when he defied them. With Paul, as with the rest of us, the important thing is not the conformity but the defiance.

In both theology and politics, we have a very long way to go before the curse on the woman is healed. But the witness of Jesus is enough to tell us that we should see the curse not as something to take for granted as an unavoidable fate, but as something which we can defy and struggle against and overcome.

The curse on the man involves the earth itself. We cannot be separated from the earth on which we stand. There is a doom upon us both. We humans experience frustration and futility; so does the earth as a whole. Just as the praise of the rest of nature requires the voice of humans to express it, so the salvation of the rest of nature requires our salvation. God's intention is to renew creation through persons, complete persons who can offer a willed response and not merely an instinctive reaction. The creation of nature and the creation of human community belong together. Human dislocation terribly inflicts dislocation on the rest of nature. At present, this is what we mainly see; our technological powers serve to increase our destructiveness. We are the worst pest on the face of the planet. So we should not be surprised if we find ourselves being frustrated by elements in nature itself.

Meanwhile, in our work, we have to battle with things and overcome obstacles. Some people live on the sunny side of the valley; at harvest time, they can see the face of God in delightful delphiniums and magnificent marrows. Others live on the shadow side, where the only things that grow well are thorns and brambles; if they are going to see the face of God at all, that is where they will have to see it. Some people's children sail through GCSEs and A levels and go on helpful journeys to Nepal or the Cameroons, and tell everyone how much they love their mothers; others just grind along, getting into trouble and having nothing much to show for it. The Christian Harvest Festival is not a competitive county show. All are welcome, whichever side of the valley they come from. Jesus took the obstructions and frustrations and they were woven into the only crown he ever wore.[2]

The proper work of Jesus, and of all who are called by him, is the fulfilment of the will and purpose of God. This includes the whole concern for renewing, reconciling and healing the world in all its sectors and communities. It includes the responsible use of the whole range of human abilities and powers, economic and spiritual, political and physical. This is the proper meaning of Christian 'vocation'.

Jesus was skilled in a particular trade. He knew the procedures involved in manufacture, he was experienced in the task of converting nature into culture, he had been disciplined by the business of purchasing raw materials and the distribution of the product. In the Hebrew Scriptures, the bread of God was manna to be simply picked up from the ground; but in the Christian inheritance, the bread of God comes through the medium of manufacture. The way by which God chooses to communicate himself to us depends on work which people do as they modify the natural creation. Manna does not have the political significance of bread. Bread tells us that nature can depend on humans for the disclosing of either its shame or its glory. 'Bread for myself is a material problem; bread for other people is a spiritual problem.'[3] The bread which we make can represent all that is most dislocated in our relationships. It can stand for the manipulations which put the simplest food beyond the buying power of the poor; it can represent the seemingly endless competition for resources, where there is not enough to go round; or it can be the eucharistic bread which is shared equally to all who are at the banquet. The eucharist is given to teach us about God and about each other and about bread and about work. It tells us that there is already an alternative to the statement that work is curse. It makes possible a new attitude of praise. And the purpose of praise, according to Waldo Williams, is 'to recreate an unblemished world'.[4]

We are dust, and to dust we shall return. In the middle age of life, one year follows another, and the idea that life goes round and round in circles makes quite good sense. At the beginning of life, things proceed from a definite beginning, and the passage of time proceeds steadily on a line, through the months in the womb, through the years up to adolescence and beyond. And, again, towards the end of life, we are back on a line. In old age, the only definite appointment I have is to die. The struggle and the sweating will be over. And this is a promise, a blessing. The most costly enterprises on which we have spent our energies are going to die. Time takes the bonds that we have tried to make, and grinds them into dust. All is vanity. Yet this was also the experience of Jesus. Most of what he did and said has been forgotten. Only a handful of his activities have been recorded, and even these seem to be strangely disconnected – a sermon here, a healing there, but with no obvious plan. The relationships with which he took most trouble collapsed utterly at the moment of final crisis.

Sent into the world to rescue the millions of mankind, to bring back the whole earth to God, his work in the end amounted to a number of separated bits and pieces – each thing in itself of course worthwhile, but without any apparent cohesion ... But in the Resurrection of Jesus, God took these bits and pieces of a disjointed ministry and wove from them a single garment of salvation for the whole world. The many and various things which Jesus did in Galilee and Judaea were not lost. They were raised with him on the first Easter morning ... Christians have been partakers of Christ's resurrection and this means that for them, as for him, nothing in human life is lost or left behind.[5]

Dust stands for the wastage of substance, the breaking down of things by the attrition of time, the grinding down of the universe into disorder. The resurrection stands for the victory over dust and wastage. This is part of what Jesus means when he says that God's will is 'that I should lose nothing of all that he has given me'.[6] It is part of what St Augustine means by stating that those who love God 'will never lose those who are dear to them, for they love them in one who is never lost'.[7] What is past is safe. It can be allowed to be put into the past. So we can feel and know that all is not wasted. It is worthwhile trying to retain integrity in a world of lies and false compromises; it is worthwhile trying to stand for justice in a situation where all the initiatives seem to be with the forces of injustice and prejudice. Death and its satellites are doomed. In the Bible's most systematic account of the meaning of resurrection, after all the sublime language about our glorious destiny and God's victory over death, Paul ends by saying, 'So, stick to what you are doing; don't be discouraged; your work in God's purposes cannot be wasted.'[8]

For us Christians, the blessing and the curse of death

remain. Death carries with it the sense that something has gone wrong. Human death, especially, is a corporate grief for the whole of humanity, because a vast proportion of our brothers and sisters in the human race die prematurely, die violently, die because the wealth of nature is so badly distributed. The land and its products are seen primarily as merchandise, not as resources for the benefit of all God's children. And that, quite literally, means death. Death is the wages of sin. And yet death also is our way of being associated with Christ and with his way of salvation for the world. We share in this death not only by our physical dying but by our commitment to Christ in this life. We die when we are baptized. The Church is a practice ground for dying. Sometimes, ordinary people seem to be much better than the Church itself at dying; the Church seems to be geared more to self-preservation than to God's programme of transformation. But for those who have had some practice in the disciplines of dying daily, the eventual death at the end of life can come with its sting withdrawn and its curse tamed. It can come as the gentle sister, as it was for St Francis, or as the last station on the road to freedom, as it was for the twentieth-century German martyr, Dietrich Bonhoeffer.[9]

*

The man named his wife Eve, because she was the mother of all living. And the Lord God made garments of skins for the man and for his wife, and clothed them. Then the Lord God said,
> *'See, the man has become like one of us, knowing good and evil; and now, he might reach out his hand and take also from the tree of life, and eat, and live forever' –*

therefore the Lord God sent him forth from the garden of

*Eden, to till the ground from which he was taken. He
drove out the man; and at the east of the garden of Eden
he placed the cherubim, and a sword flaming and turning
to guard the way to the tree of life.*

Genesis 3:20–24

The man and woman have no reply to make to God. But the
man turns to the woman and sees that a change is needed.
Up to now, her name has been 'Woman'; now he gives her
the name 'Eve', which is understood to refer to her role as
mother. We now think of 'Eve' as her real name. But actually, in giving this name, Adam diverts attention away from
the relationship of the woman to himself and on to a function which she is going to perform. 'Mother' is a powerful
name; it is a name of hope, and it is rightly built early into
the fabric of the story. Nevertheless, in this context, it is
a poorer name than 'woman'; there is no ecstasy in it, no
passionate recognition. In giving her this name, the man is
pushing her identity away from himself. 'Woman' is a
uniquely human word; 'Mother', in spite of all its power
and value, is not.

God gives clothes. He accepts the woman and man as
they are; he recognizes that they feel the need for proper
covering. The clothes are not a disguise; in our disunited
condition, we feel that we need an appropriate privacy.
Truthfulness does not mean that everything has to be pub-
licized. If we publicize something that is properly private,
we are liars, however accurate our words may be. The provision of concealment is part of preservation, a blessing.
God does not allow our stupidity to limit his mercy. It
would make good sense if he punished the woman and
man by exposing them, by tearing off the feeble attempt at
covering which they had made for themselves. But he does

for them what they have not succeeded in doing for themselves. He supplies equipment for their preservation; he shows that he is not bound to the past. He is not prepared to allow their offence to be the last word about them. This is forgiveness. It looks wrong. It looks as if the guilty are being treated as innocent. But God's justifying of the guilty is not a legal deception; it is a refusal to treat the guilt as being the most important thing about the person.

If the man and woman have been foolish enough to grasp the fruit of the tree of knowledge, they may be tempted to go back and try to stave off the threat of death by grasping the fruit of the tree of life. In his mercy, God makes this impossible. Life is not to be grabbed like this. The blessing of death is not to be avoided by either the selfish virtue of the good or the misplaced skill of the clever. Though it appeared to him in its worst form, death was not avoided by the Son of God himself. He has made a way to the tree of life by another way, not by avoiding death but by accepting it. The life that we might hope for by avoiding death is the life of the old. That is what people are paying for when they give instructions for their corpses to be frozen. Christ's rising to new life was not an achievement of medical technology. It was the gift of the Creator, given to one who had been crucified, put to death as a result of the combined decision of religion, state, and public opinion. Christ was crucified by the common consent of those who wanted him to be killed as a terrorist, and treated as unwanted, unnecessary, redundant, surplus to the world's requirements. The life that comes through Christ comes not through the prolongation of the old, not by the selection of the best of the old, but by the death of the old. The way to the tree of life is through association with Christ, who was treated as rubbish by the best law and the best religion of the world.

So Adam is sent out of the garden. Eve, as is clear from the story as it develops later, remains his wife and companion. They go into the area that is limited by death. Our normal shorthand word for this is 'history'. Whatever else may or may not happen, the most basic shaper of history is the fact of death; without it, history as we know it simply would not be. 'Adam' is the name given to the first creature who was capable of bearing responsibility for his choices; he belongs to history. But Adam's story is also universal. Jesus Christ is the name of the first to be raised from the dead; he also belongs to history. But our primary message is not that Jesus rose from the dead in AD 32 but that he is risen today. The other characters in the Hebrew Scriptures are of history, of humanity's past experience; in the same way, the Apostles are of history: they are our ancestors in the Christian movement. But we meet God insofar as we ourselves *are* Adam, and insofar as we ourselves *are* the Body of Christ.

God's original purpose is obstructed by human disorder. But God is not discouraged. He is God of the second chance, and he gives himself a second chance. Creation involves finding a new way. God, the Creator at work, is the supreme improviser. He has given freedom to his creatures. He keeps freedom for himself. Christians usually call this story 'the Fall'. But there is nothing in the text that requires this title. Some Jews see the story as a story of emancipation or liberation. God has to learn how to be God in a new way; he has to learn how to work with a human creation which, for better or worse, has claimed some freedom. Freedom is like love; if there is real love, or real freedom, there is more to come.

The story in chapters 2 and 3 is a very old part of the Bible; it was written before chapter 1. Perhaps chapter 1 was devised to put the balance right, to correct the impression given by chapters 2 and 3 (and 4), that Creation led only to disaster and murder. We can pinpoint three stages: first, chapters 2 and 3, which tell of experiments and disappointments; then chapter 1, which defiantly insists that, whatever the evidence to the contrary, creation is a blessing; and finally the Christian gospel, which says that God uses his freedom to become part of his creation, claiming that human life is an authentic way of life for the divine, claiming that the world and all that is in it is good and worthy to be loved and healed.

'As in Adam all die ...' There is indeed a doom on the human race. We never can get things right for long. Our best endeavours become corrupted by selfishness or stupidity. We try to separate ourselves from the common herd. We look for devices to save us from death, misery, despair, ignorance, poverty, frustration. We grasp things which give us hope of being superior, by being richer, wiser, more attractive, more successful, more morally virtuous. To be credible, this sort of salvation has to be for a minority. The majority will be a failure so that we can feel that we can be a success. Even within the family of God, there have been many who have found it difficult to realize that we have our place in it not by grasping or achieving but by accepting a gift. There have been, and still are, Christians who, deep down, believe that God looks with more favour on people who live good lives and succeed in keeping the rules, and that those who go in for intellectual and spiritual exercises will be closer to heaven than those who live in the mess and muck of material things. This goes close to the ancient heresy called Pelagianism. Pelagius, in the fifth century of Christianity, was accused of teaching that human beings could achieve holiness without total dependence on God, that they could grasp it individually for themselves rather than receive it as a gift with other people. So those who start off with the advantage of intellectual and spiritual inclinations, and who have privileged positions in which to use them, will end up closest to God. This kind of outlook splits up the unity of creation. It divides the spiritual from the material, the religious from the political. We begin to think that we are nearer to God if we are spirit *minus* matter – which is exactly the opposite of God's action of incarnation. It splits off the material kind of person from the spiritual kind of person. It gives second-class citizenship to the whole female sex, whose physical and emotional rhythms are not so easily detached from intellectual and spiritual life as those of the male. It puts at a disadvantage those who, whether by personal preference or by social origin, find themselves earning their living by manual rather than intellectual skills. Holiness becomes defined by those who have the opportunity and inclination for certain types of prayer and who have a personality-shape to match. This sort of heresy is not a mere intellectual mistake. I do not know of any account of this heresy by a professional theologian that goes so clearly to the heart of the matter as that of Saunders Lewis, the Welsh politician and playwright. He wrote a play about St Germanus, the leader of the struggle against Pelagianism in Britain (in Wales all the churches called Llanarmon are dedicated in the name of Germanus, so they should be especially keen to maintain his teaching!). This is Germanus's key speech:

How can we guard the city,
what commonalty will we achieve,
what building together in love and what guarding
    together,
if we be not one in Adam and one in Christ?
And this is the harm the Pelagians do,
they break the unity we have in nature and our new
    unity through grace
so that the lettered man is not of one nation with the
    poor man,
but acquires by his own effort his own heaven
in unshakeable self-satisfaction.[10]

The translation above is from a letter to me from Saunders Lewis in 1977, in which he explains the background to the play. He wrote it in 1937, while he and two colleagues were awaiting their final trial for setting fire to a military installation near Pwllheli. 'It was a time of severe slump and unemployment, and in Swansea and in Merthyr I had for some three years been working with the unemployed and had got University College Swansea to co-operate in arranging extension lectures for the young out-of-work. But the majority of teachers in the Welsh University were little concerned ... They, while the out-of-work were rotting in hopeless hell, were very placidly enjoying their scholarly security.' The ancient heresy, therefore, has an immediate significance. It represents the refusal of the scholar to see his solidarity with the peasant. And the answer to it is that we are one race, one in Adam and one in Christ.

In Adam, all die. But the Christian gospel does not save us by detaching us from Adam. It does not give Christians special favour, in contrast to the rest of the human race. What it does say is that God has chosen one person for the sake of the whole of the rest of the human race. God has provided a new Adam. 'As in Adam all die, so in Christ shall all be made alive.'[11] The second 'all' cannot be narrower in intention than the first 'all'. In Christ, we can be in solidarity with the rest of the human race and still get salvation; indeed, it is only in solidarity with the rest of the human race that we can be saved. This is the effect of what Christ has done for us in history. It is the new creation. We can affirm this truth or deny it; we can conceal it or reveal it. But we cannot create it, for it is already achieved in the work of Christ; and we cannot destroy it, for it is the central purpose of the eternal God.

Adam is expelled from Paradise into the ordinary world. He is given a task: to till the earth out of which he has been made. He is to take responsibility for the well-being of the earth – the same task as is given to the human beings in the account of the first chapter of Genesis.

Adam and Eve are dispossessed. They are not un-employed, nor are they entirely homeless; but in their experience they represent the millions of people who find themselves exiled and uprooted. The ex-slaves who first treasured the story would recognize their situation only too well. 'Redemption' means being given space, being taken out of a situation where one is valued only in terms of one's productivity; it means being set free. The first Adam is re-instated by the new Adam, the Redeemer.

People who have known oppression and enslavement need, more than most people, to hear the whole story and not just the 'Christian' bit. They need to see themselves within a total pattern of history. A great African preacher, Michael Mzobe, once gave a long sermon in which he described the story of human disorder, throughout history, through the eyes of Adam, who has been given a grand-stand view of the world. Adam suffers at every stage, seeing the way in which his first act of disobedience is mirrored and replicated in the cruelties and faithlessness of human beings all down the ages. But the whole point of the sermon is to describe the joy when he sees Christ giving to the Father the good news of the victory won on Easter Day. Adam is reinstated; the poor exile is given new status by the new Adam, himself poor among the poor, non-citizen among the non-citizens. In the first days of our movement, it was the dispossessed across the Roman Empire who saw the point and accepted the message in their thousands. It is impossible to preach the full message of Easter without going back to the beginning. Genesis must be part of the gospel.[12]

So Adam is cast out, and God takes special steps to make sure that he will not be able to grab the fruit of the tree of life.

The language about angels and cherubim has become badly worn for us. We have got so used to some kinds of pictures of them – anatomically impossible creatures with wings, or chubby little children – that it is difficult to believe in their reality. Here, at the first appearance of an angel in the Bible, we have a corrective. The angel is a spiritual power with a specific task. It stands for the human experience of being excluded, by a power stronger than any individual human power. This is a grievous experience, as anyone can tell who has been exiled. The angel stands for this experience, at its most personal and frightening. Nowadays, we might prefer to use an abstract noun, such as 'public opinion' or 'the system'. In the Bible, angels are usually seen as alarming, even when they are under the direct instructions of God. Whatever we care to call them, there are superhuman powers at large in the world; at their worst they captivate the human spirit and cause people to be far more evil in their groups than they would be as individuals. This is the effect, for instance, of racial prejudice or of traditional enmities. St Paul knew very well that an angel of religious exclusiveness and enthusiasm could destroy a person; but Christ has met and mastered these powers on the cross, and brought them into subjection to himself.[13]

The sword, whirling and flashing, seems to have a life of its own. Perhaps it is an image drawn from lightning, which is a most powerful force for keeping a person feeling insecure and immobile. Just when the storm seems to have shifted, the lightning suddenly jumps back, as if to say, 'Get back behind the line; you can't play tricks with me.'

The barring of the way to the tree of life is a preservation and a blessing. But it is also punishment. God is angry. His speech is left half-finished; the creating word finds himself lost for words. This is a sign of God's anger, and there is no anger without emotion. But, unlike most of our anger, God's anger does not arise from unlovedness but from love.

God's anger will not ease until we allow ourselves to grow into the full person that we are designed to be. As Judge, he compares what we are with what we could be, our actual with our potential. As Saviour, he places obstacles in our way when we seek to get the fruit by trying to grasp it, to achieve it for ourselves by setting ourselves in competition with others. As Creator, he knows how he has made us and what we are capable of. God creates what he judges and saves; God judges what he creates and saves. God saves what he creates and judges. Creator, Judge and Saviour are one God. And Christ has the right to be our Judge, because he himself has been on the receiving end of human judgement. He knows what it is to be convicted and sentenced by human verdict. He was excluded, deported from the city, hanged outside the city wall. Even when we are judged, he is on our side.

We look from the beginning of the Bible to its end. The Bible begins in a garden but ends in a city. Our hope is not to return to the womb, to the joys of a fabulous golden age in the past. Our hope is not for the clock to be put back, or for history to be reversed. Our origin is described in terms of natural imagery; our destiny is described in terms of political imagery. Political action will not, in itself, bring about the Kingdom of God, but it is in terms of political structure rather than biological process that we can tell how far off we are from our destiny, how near we are to our design.[14]

In the city of God, as in the garden, the tree of life is in the middle. There are two trees, both drawing sustenance from the water of life and making it available to the nations. They are nourishing and healing. They represent the purpose of God to make humanity whole, and to make all creation whole. God is worshipped by the innumerable throng of people who are moving out of their nations, out of their groups of ancestral and cultural origin, into a single community of adoration.[15] But their diversity is not over-ruled. The city is a complex community of diverse individuals. Each person in the final community has a specific identity as a child of God.

For Adam and for the whole human race, the way to the tree of life is not opened by individual defiance of the angel or the sword, but by sharing in the community of Christ, who has overcome death and all that separates human beings from each other. That is the vision of the heavenly Jerusalem, our true citizenship, which is beyond time and space. This is the model for our citizenship on earth. The earthly Jerusalem remains, very much part of time and space. In its present tragedy, it stands for the inability of human beings to accept each other, to put the past into the past, and to honour each other as children of Adam. Christians owe this whole story to our older cousins, the Jews. Jesus was a Jew, a member of the people who gave us Genesis. Jesus was a human being, identified with all who bear the human form. Jesus was a mammal, a product of the evolutionary process which has enabled the emergence of all life. Jesus' body, like yours and mine, consisted of the dust of dead stars. We may have different theologies about him, but Jesus belongs to us all, and most especially to the grieving communities of the present Jerusalem – Jew, Christian, Muslim – who all claim the Genesis story.

Adam died. A tradition developed that his skull was buried at 'a place called the place of a skull, which is called in the Hebrew Golgotha'.[16] There was set up another tree, outside the walls of that city, at a specific place, at a specific time, under Pontius Pilate. Set in the middle of space and history, the cross is for us the tree of truth and the tree of life. It is the sign that we can be associated with the Lord of life by being associated with him in his death. But it is also the sign of healing, for the one who is lifted up on the tree is drawing all people to himself and so to each other.

This whole story has been about me, for I am Adam. If that is not so, his story is an idle diversion, and I need not bother about it. Christ has come to take us and break us and remake us; his story, also, is about me. If Christ also is not me, I need not bother about him; his story also is an idle diversion if I am not identified with him, not because I am divine like him but because he is human like me.

We think that Paradise and Calvary,
Christ's Cross and Adam's tree, stood in one place;
Look, Lord, and find both Adams met in me;
As the first Adam's sweat surrounds my face,
May the last Adam's blood my soul embrace.[17]

For Reflection

Do you know of a place where there is a notice saying, 'Keep Out', 'Admittance to Authorized Personnel only', or some such barrier? Spend some time being there. Keep company with all who are excluded, on account of their race, their disability, their sexual orientation, their unacceptable behaviour, their religious affiliation, or whatever. On which side of the barrier is Christ?

Questions for Working Groups

1. Is your local church mainly in business to change and transform, or to preserve things and keep them as they are? Which do you really want for yourself?

2. This programme of study has been about God at work, especially in his enterprise of creation. Have

you recognized some ways in which God is at work in his world now?

3. Do you reckon that your church helps to put people at a distance from each other? Or does it truly bring people together by helping to cross boundaries? In practice, to whom do you feel you have been brought nearer through your involvement with the Church? How far do you feel that this has had any effect on the world around?

4. Look back over your meetings together. Are there any matters which you want to refer to other groups, to your church leadership, to local authorities or other organizations? Try to make sure that you don't lose insights, ideas or recommendations which you have been given.

Notes and References

Although I make no direct quotations from it, my whole approach in this book owes a great deal to Dietrich Bonhoeffer, *Creation and Fall* (SCM Press, London, 1959).

For their advice and critical encouragement, I am grateful to my wife, Shirley, and to Dr Trevor Churchman of St Asaph Cathedral.

Introduction

1. John Davies, *Beginning Now* (Collins, London, 1971).
2. According to the Church Urban Fund, there were 150,000 homeless people in Britain in 1999.
3. David Jones, *The Anathemata* (Faber & Faber, London, 1972); R.S. Thomas, *Later Poems* (Macmillan, London, 1983); and subsequent collections.

Chapter 1

1. Augustine, *Confessions* (trans. R.S. Pine-Coffin; Penguin, Harmondsworth, 1961), pp. 262ff.
2. See Patrick Thomas, *Candle in the Darkness* (Gwasg Gomer, Llandysul, 1997), pp. 70, 91, 107.
3. Exodus 20:21.
4. David Jones, *The Sleeping Lord* (Faber & Faber Ltd, London, 1974), p. 63. Quoted by permission of the publishers.
5. Mark 4:1–34; John 12:24; 1 Corinthians 12:35–44.

Chapter 2

1. John Polkinghorne, *Science and Christian Belief* (SPCK, London, 1994), p. 72.

2. See John Davies, *Be Born in Us Today* (Canterbury Press, Norwich, 1999), pp. 136–53.

3. See Angela Tilby, *Science and the Soul* (SPCK , London, 1992), p. 30.

4. *The Cloud of Unknowing* (trans. Clifton Wolters; Penguin, Harmondsworth, 1961), pp. 128–29.

5. Stephen W. Hawking *A Brief History of Time* (Transworld Publications, London, 1988), p. 125.

6. Paul Davies, *God and the New Physics* (Penguin, Harmondsworth, 1986), p. 179.

7. Paul Gerhardt, 'The Duteous Day Now Closeth', no. 278 in *English Hymnal*.

Chapter 3

1. Eric Gill, *Last Essays* (Jonathan Cape, London, 1942), p. 14. There is a good example of the beauty and clarity of his lettering in the War Memorial that he made at Chirk.

2. Exodus 31:2.

3. See Dorothy L. Sayers, *The Mind of the Maker* (Methuen, London, 1941), pp. 22–46. Also John Thurmer, *Reluctant Evangelist* (Dorothy L. Sayers Society, Hurstpierpoint, 1996).

4. See Doug Alker, *Really Not Interested in the Deaf?* (D. Alker, Darwen, 2000).

5. See 'Ten Golden Rules for Teaching New Songs', in John Bell, *Innkeepers and Light Sleepers* (Wild Goose Publications, Glasgow, 1992), p. 57.

6. Colossians 1:15; Philippians 2:6–8.

7. Theodosius Dobzhansky, *The Biological Basis of Human Freedom* (Columbia University Press, New York, 1954), p. 56.

8. T.H. White, *The Sword in the Stone* (Collins, London, 1950), p. 314.

9. The Welsh language has a similar vocabulary at this point. The same word 'meddwl' is used as a verb, corresponding to 'think', and as a noun, corresponding to 'mind'.

10. See C. Deane-Drummond, *Genetic Engineering for a New Earth?* (Grove Books, Cambridge, 1999).

11. Deuteronomy 26:1–13 (too often, when this passage is used as a lesson at Harvest, the last three verses are omitted).

12. Quoted in *Celebrating One World* (CAFOD and St Thomas More Centre, London, 1989), p. 78.

Chapter 4

1. Exodus 20:10; Deuteronomy 5:14–15.
2. Deuteronomy 31:10–13; Exodus: 23:1–9.
3. Leviticus 25:8–43.
4. Quotations from J.P. Miranda, *Marx and the Bible* (Orbis Books, New York, 1974), pp. 15ff.; and K. Leech, *True God* (Sheldon Press, London, 1980), p. 414.
5. Amos 8:4–6.
6. John Polkinghorne, *Reason and Reality* (SPCK, London, 1991), p. 71.
7. From the Apocrypha in most Bibles, under the title 'Song of the three holy children'. There are two modern versions in *Hymns for Today's Church* (Hodder & Stoughton, London, 1987), nos. 604 and S32.
8. Taken from *God's Presence Makes the World* by A. M. Allchin, published and copyright 1971 by Darton, Longman & Todd Ltd, and used by permission of the publishers.

Chapter 5

1. Quoted in C.A. Coulson, *Science and Christian Belief* (Collins, London, 1958), p. 80.
2. John 20:28.
3. Mark 4:9.
4. Dobzhansky, *The Biological Basis of Human Freedom*, p. 13.
5. E.g. Jonah; Psalm 107:23–32.
6. Nelson Mandela, *Long Walk to Freedom* (Little, Brown, London, 1994), p. 476.
7. Luke 23:43.
8. *The Poems of Wilfred Owen* (ed. Jon Stallworthy; Hogarth Press, London, 1985), p. 126.

Chapter 6

1. D. Bonhoeffer, *Life Together* (SCM Press, London, 1954), pp. 66–67.

2. Acts 8:26–40.
3. H. Butterfield, *The Origins of Modern Science* (G. Bell, London, 1965), p. 221.
4. Hebrews 11:8–10; and note many occasions when Jesus comments on someone's 'faith'.
5. 1 Corinthians 11:8–12.
6. 1 Corinthians 13:6.
7. Matthew 19:5.

Chapter 7

1. Numbers 21:6, 9; Isaiah 6:2; 2 Kings 18:4; John 3:14.
2. Isaiah 40:25.
3. Matthew 7:24
4. Exodus 32:4.
5. T.H. Huxley, *Evolution and Ethics* (Macmillan, London, 1903), p. 83.
6. E.g. Mark 3:13–19; Matthew 21:14–16; Luke 15:1–2.
7. Luke 19:41–42.
8. John 18:3; Luke 23:12; Mark 12:13.
9. E.W. Southcott, *The Parish Comes Alive* (Mowbray, Oxford, 1956), p. 43.
10. Luke 7:36–50; John 8:1–11.
11. Howard Thurman, *Jesus and the Disinherited* (Abingdon, Nashville, 1949), p. 77.
12. Matthew 14:36.
13. Matthew 22:11–14.
14. Luke 15:1–2, 11–31.
15. Mark 2:12; John 9:1–38.

Chapter 8

1. Colossians 2:16–23; 2 Timothy 2:16–26, for example.
2. For a superbly passionate interpretation of this theme, see the story by E. Tegla Davies, *Samuel Jones's Harvest Thanksgiving* (*Cwrdd Diolchgarwch Samuel Jones yr Hendre*) in Gwyn Jones and Islwyn Ffowc Elis (eds.), *Twenty-Five Welsh Short Stories* (OUP, London, 1971), pp. 189ff.
3. Nicholas Berdyaev, quoted in J.A.T. Robinson *On Being the Church in the World* (SCM Press, London), p. 35.

4. A.M. Allchin, *Praise Above All* (University of Wales Press, Cardiff, 1991), p. 3.

5. H.A. Williams, *Jesus and the Resurrection*, (Longmans, Green, London, 1951), pp. 66ff.

6. John 6:39.

7. Augustine, *Confessions*, p. 79.

8. 1 Corinthians 15:58.

9. See St Francis, *Canticle of Brother Sun*; and D. Bonhoeffer, *Letters and Papers from Prison* (ET; SCM Press, London, 1953), p. 176.

10. From the play *Buchedd Garmon* (*The Life of Germanus*) (Gwasg Aberystwyth, 1937) (my italics).

11. 1 Corinthians 15:22.

12. B. Sundkler, *The Christian Ministry in Africa* (SCM Press, London, 1960), p. 283.

13. Colossians 2:15.

14. Revelation 21; Galatians 4:26.

15. Revelation 7:9–10.

16. Mark 15:22

17. John Donne, *Hymn to God my God, in my Sicknesse*.